'Here is a landmark book on the identity, nature,
Bible in God's economy of salvation and revelation. It combines
a biblical theology of the Bible, the relationship between God
the Trinity and the Bible, key doctrinal beliefs about the Bible, and
a practical theology of the Bible as read and preached. It shows
how our faithful worship of God must include paying close
attention to the Bible. A splendid addition to IVP publications.
I thank God for it.'
Peter Adam

'Judicious, lucid, fresh, incisive, and above all Scripture-driven, this
is a splendid book. I found my thinking continually refined and
sharpened as I read.'
Julian Hardyman

'A very fine treatment of the classical Christian doctrine of Holy
Scripture, which draws particularly on the theological wisdom of
the Reformed tradition. A particular strength of the book is the
way in which the author formulates his account of Scripture from
Scripture itself, notably from its covenantal character. *Words of
Life* is well-written and clear-headed, thoughtful and judicious.'
Paul Helm

'This is an important book, which demonstrates the indispensable
union of the Word of God and the Spirit of God, to accomplish
the work of God. It will deepen confidence in the Bible's
authority and competence in handling its contents, through its
wide-ranging historical survey and up-to-date contemporary
applications. A book to renew confidence that the Bible is the
cutting-edge of Christian resurgence and growth.'
David Jackman

'This is both a great read and a sterling work of scholarship. It is comprehensive in scope, rich in historical awareness and acute in critique. It respects the past without idolising it, draws discriminatingly on modern speech-theory, offers fine insights into the relation between scripture and tradition and gives a judicious assessment of inerrancy. Text-book and treat in a single volume!'
Donald Macleod

'Timothy Ward's exposition of the nature and place of the Bible is well-informed and thoroughly thought through. It is a product of alert contemporary awareness, deep-level theological discernment, and mature personal judgment. Rarely has a book on this subject stirred me to such emphatic agreement and admiration.'
J. I. Packer

'At last, a primer on the doctrine of Scripture that is brilliantly conceived, academically aware and beautifully written. Tim Ward scores highly because he carefully establishes the biblical and theological underpinnings of his subject before examining traditional doctrinal categories. The discussions on inerrancy, *sola scriptura* and preaching are particularly stimulating and worthwhile. Without question, this is a significant addition to the literature.'
Jonathan Stephen

Words of Life

SCRIPTURE AS THE LIVING AND ACTIVE WORD OF GOD

TIMOTHY WARD

IVP Academic

An imprint of InterVarsity Press
Downers Grove, Illinois

InterVarsity Press
P.O. Box 1400, Downers Grove, IL 60515-1426
Internet: www.ivpress.com
E-mail: email@ivpress.com

InterVarsity Press® is the book-publishing division of InterVarsity Christian Fellowship/USA®, a movement of students and faculty active on campus at hundreds of universities, colleges and schools of nursing in the United States of America, and a member movement of the International Fellowship of Evangelical Students. For information about local and regional activities, write Public Relations Dept., InterVarsity Christian Fellowship/USA, 6400 Schroeder Rd., P.O. Box 7895, Madison, WI 53707-7895, or visit the IVCF website at <www.intervarsity.org>.

ISBN 978-0-8308-2744-2

Printed in the United States of America ∞

 InterVarsity Press is committed to protecting the environment and to the responsible use of natural resources. As a member of Green Press Initiative we use recycled paper whenever possible. To learn more about the Green Press Initiative, visit <www.greenpressinitiative.org>.

Library of Congress Cataloging-in-Publication Data

A catalog record for this book is available from the Library of Congress.

P	20	19	18	17	16	15	14	13	12	11	10	9	8	7	6	5	4	3	2	1
Y	26	25	24	23	22	21	20	19	18	17	16	15	14	13	12	11	10	09			

CONTENTS

Acknowledgments   7

1. **Introduction: God and the Bible**   9

2. **God and Scripture: a biblical outline**   20

    God's action and his words   20
        The Old Testament   20
        The New Testament   25
    God's person and his words   26
    God's words and human words   32
    Christ's words, and God's action and person   37
    Christ's words and human words   40
    God's words and the Bible   43

3. **The Trinity and Scripture: a theological outline**   49

    The Father and Scripture: the covenant book   51
        Redemption and Scripture   52
        Revelation and Scripture   60
    The Son and Scripture: the words of the Word   67
        Jesus and the Bible as both 'Word of God'   67
        Scripture and the incarnation   74
    The Holy Spirit and Scripture: the God-breathed Word   78
        The inspiration of Scripture   79

The preservation of Scripture   89
The illumination of Scripture   92
Summary   94

4. **The attributes of Scripture: a doctrinal outline**   96

The necessity of Scripture   98
The sufficiency of Scripture   106
The clarity of Scripture   115
    Preaching and a clear Bible   121
    Diverse interpretations and a clear Bible   122
    Defining the clarity of Scripture   124
The authority of Scripture   127
    The nature of biblical authority   127
    Inerrancy and infallibility   130

5. **The Bible and Christian life: the doctrine of
    Scripture applied**   141

The meaning of *sola scriptura*   141
Scripture and the Christian community   151
Scripture and preaching   156
    The Spirit and the Bible   160
    The Spirit and the preacher   163
    The Spirit and the people of God   168
Scripture and the individual Christian   170
    Private Bible reading in relation to corporate
        Bible reading and preaching   171
    The aim of Bible reading   174

6. **Summary**   177

Index of ancient and modern authors   180
Index of biblical references   182

ACKNOWLEDGMENTS

I am very grateful to the many people who have taught me much about God and his Word over the years. A few of those, as well as others who have interacted with my own teaching on this topic in several different settings, may find their own insights unwittingly passed off here as my own. I can only apologize for my forgetfulness, and gladly acknowledge my debt to them here. Some readers of this book will notice the continuing academic influence of my doctoral supervisor, Professor Kevin Vanhoozer. I remain thankful to him for all that he contributed to me. David Gibson, Tim Oglesby and Judi Oglesby generously took the time to read the manuscript and made excellent suggestions for improving it. Phil Duce at IVP has proved to be a patient and encouraging editor, for which I am very grateful. The church family at Holy Trinity Church in Hinckley, of which I am a part, provide a great setting in which to live and serve. I trust that this book is one small sign for them that 'sabbatical' does not just mean 'holiday'!

I also want to thank my son, Jonathan, for not letting me forget that I am supposed to be playing Daddy as well as working Daddy. To my wife, Erica, must go deep thankfulness for her devoted love and patience, and for gently pointing out to me that a book does not get written unless you stop sitting around talking about it, and actually get on and write it.

All quotations from the Bible are from Today's New International Version.

Earlier versions of some parts of this book have been previously published in the following volumes, and this material is used with the permission of the publishers:

1. *Word and Supplement: Speech Acts, Biblical Texts and the Sufficiency of Scripture* (Oxford: Oxford University Press, 2002).
2. 'The Incarnation and Scripture', in David Peterson (ed.), *The Word Became Flesh: Evangelicals and the Incarnation* (Carlisle: Paternoster, 2003), pp. 152–184.
3. 'The Sufficiency of Scripture', in Lynn Quigley (ed.), *Reformed Theology in Contemporary Perspective: Westminster: Yesterday, Today – and Tomorrow?* (Edinburgh: Rutherford House, 2006), pp. 10–45.
4. 'Proclamation in the Power of the Spirit', in David F. Wright (ed.), *Spirit of Truth and Power* (Edinburgh: Rutherford House, 2001).

1. INTRODUCTION: GOD AND THE BIBLE

In my own Anglican denomination it has long been customary, at the end of the public reading of Scripture, for the reader to say, 'This is the Word of the Lord.' Throughout Christian history, the overwhelmingly predominant view of the Bible has been that it is itself the living and active Word of God. To say that the Bible is the Word of God is to say, putting it another way, that 'what the Bible says, God says'. In this book I shall refer to this view of the Bible in different ways: as the evangelical view of Scripture, or as the view held by the Protestant Reformers of the sixteenth century, or sometimes as the orthodox view. When I talk in these ways, however, those different labels ought not to obscure the fact that the conviction most commonly held about the Bible by Christians has been, and is, that it is the *Word of God*.

However, this is not always an easy view of the Bible to defend in the face of critics, or to understand properly for oneself. I once saw a pencil-drawn cartoon that depicted a man, alone in a bare room, sitting on an uncomfortable-looking chair. Open on his lap was a ridiculously oversized book, and the book's title was visible, written on the spine: 'Brief Notes on Leviticus'. He was studying the book intently, and was frankly looking pretty serious and dour. The caption underneath read, 'Chris the Calvinist just lived for pleasure'.

I know this is only a cartoon (and am ignoring the cheap shot it makes about Calvinists, among whom I would want to identify myself!). Yet it does put its finger on a worry about the Bible that lies not far below the surface for many Christians. Indeed for some people this is a worry that long ago broke through the surface, and that they have had to face explicitly. It is at heart the worry that, if we insist the Bible is itself God's Word, we might pay so much attention to Scripture that we fail to pay all the attention we should to Christ. And that would be a very serious mistake to make, tantamount to the sin of idolatry (or, as it is sometimes called in this case, 'bibliolatry': worship of the book). We often like to think our concerns and questions are brand new ones, but of course that is rarely the case. This worry about the Bible and Christ has been thought through for centuries, as we shall come to see.

The same basic question can be asked in many different ways: Does the fullness of life which Christ came to bring really have to involve paying such close attention to the Bible? Does our new life in the Spirit really need to be centred around what seem to be comprehension exercises on biblical texts? Has a high view of Scripture led some of us to turn our weekly gatherings for worship into little more than preaching rallies, where we sit passively, when in fact our meetings should be joyful, collaborative and encouraging? Surely Christ came to call us to be disciples, not bookworms? Indeed did Jesus not reserve some of his harshest criticisms for groups such as the Pharisees and teachers of the law, taking them to task for being obsessed with rightly interpreting tiny details of Scripture, while missing the great spiritual realities to which Scripture was pointing them? Is the evangelical view of Scripture in the end therefore fundamentally Pharisaic, and not really fully Christian?

The biblical scholar John Barton, who wishes to build on these worries in order to encourage people away from the evangelical view of Scripture, has put it this way:

it is not primarily the Bible that is the Word of God, but Jesus Christ. I do not think one could find a single Christian who would dissent from this proposition, for to do so would plainly be to commit what is sometimes called bibliolatry: the elevation of the Bible above Christ himself. . . . Christians are not those who believe in the Bible, but those who believe in Christ.[1]

It is easy to find Christians who say they have abandoned the evangelical doctrine of Scripture because they have found this kind of argument persuasive. (In some places, such people have terms like 'open evangelical' and 'post-conservative' to describe themselves.) Indeed it can seem impossible, at first, to disagree with this quotation from Barton. Christians certainly are in relationship with a saviour, not with a paper-and-ink book. Our devotion should be towards a living Lord, not to words printed on a page. Of course many Christians, looking again at Barton's words, would soon realize that in the last sentence he is forcing a false dichotomy on us. We do not have to choose between 'believing in the Bible' and 'believing in Christ'. As Christians we are called on to do *both*. In fact one crucial means by which we demonstrate our faith in Christ is by also believing what the Bible says. Perhaps the most straightforward argument for this begins by observing the fact that Jesus himself treated the Jewish Scriptures, our Old Testament, as themselves words from God, and so if we are going to be devoted to him then we must make sure our view of the Scriptures is the same as his.[2]

This gets us to the heart of what I am attempting to do in this book: I want to articulate, explain and defend what we are really saying when we proclaim, as we must, that the Bible is God's Word. In particular, this is how I want to go about this: *I am attempting to describe the nature of the relationship between God and Scripture.* Why is it the case that, in order to worship God faithfully, we need to pay close attention to the Bible? Why is it the case that,

---

1. John Barton, *People of the Book? The Authority of the Bible in Christianity* (London: SPCK, 1988), pp. 81, 83.
2. A classic (and still very helpful) exposition of Christ's high view of the Old Testament is found in John Wenham, *Christ and the Bible* (Guildford, Surrey: Eagle, 1993).

in order to be a faithful disciple of the Word-made-flesh, I need to base my life on the words of Scripture? Why is it the case that, in order to walk in step with the Spirit, I need to trust and obey what Scripture says? And how can we do all of this without beginning to worship a book instead of the Lord? What I am offering here, then, is *an outline of what is usually called the doctrine of Scripture.*

The outline has three main components, each building on what comes previously. The first is *a biblical outline.* We shall look within the Bible itself, in order to discern the Bible's own description of the relationship between, on the one hand, God and Christ, and, on the other hand, the words by which they speak and act. To give a very brief summary in advance: we shall find that the words of the Bible are a significant aspect of *God's action* in the world. The relationship between God and the Bible is at heart to do with the actions God uses the Bible to perform. (The word of God is, after all, living and *active*, according to Heb. 4:12.)

It is important that we start in this way with a biblical outline, for too often writing on the doctrine of Scripture, whether supportive or critical of the evangelical view of Scripture, has started elsewhere than with the biblical shape of God's acts of speech. This shape is that of the history of God's revelatory and redemptive activity in the world. It is focused initially on his covenant people in Israel, and then comes to a climax in the birth, death, resurrection and ascension of his Son, the Word made flesh, before spreading out to the whole world through the outpouring of the Holy Spirit and the proclamation of the gospel. Claims that 'the Bible is the Word of God' must be explicitly related to God's speech and actions in this history.

Writing on Scripture that does not take account of this usually runs into trouble of one kind or another. Examples of this can be found in consciously evangelical writing that wants primarily to defend one or another historic formulation of the doctrine of Scripture, without seriously reflecting on the areas where that formulation might need reconsidering in the light of Scripture. However, a hallmark of Protestant theology ought always to be its adherence to the Reformation maxim *ecclesia semper reformanda* (the church is always in need of reforming). Other writers have approached Scripture from a theological or doctrinal starting

point. Such works can give real insights, but lack the explicit biblical moorings each aspect of the doctrine of Scripture requires in
order to demonstrate that it is not just coherent within systematic
theology, but also that it is in genuine conformity with the content
of the very book it intends to describe, and with the actions of the
God revealed in that book.[3] Still other writers have begun their
work on Scripture with categories drawn from outside Scripture
and theology, usually with the apologetic aim of updating the doctrine of Scripture in order to make it more comprehensible (and,
in some cases, apparently more credible) to a new generation in a
new culture.[4] The explicitly biblical foundation I shall lay aims to
avoid some of these problems.

Following this biblical outline, I shall begin to draw the
threads together into *a theological outline of Scripture in its relationship
with God*, focusing on Scripture's role in relationship with each of
the persons of the Trinity. In the construction of any aspect of
Christian doctrine it is appropriate to move in this way from an
analysis of the biblical material to a theological exposition of
that material. However, it is especially important to make these
theological steps explicit here, because of the history of the

---

3. I think here most recently of John Webster's stimulating *Holy Scripture: A
   Dogmatic Sketch* (Cambridge: Cambridge University Press, 2003).

4. I think here particularly of the work on inspiration by William Abraham,
   which, while retaining the word 'inspiration', long used in evangelical
   doctrines of Scripture, in effect redefines the theological use of that
   term according to its regular use in vernacular non-theological contexts
   (William Abraham, *The Divine Inspiration of Holy Scripture* [Oxford:
   Oxford University Press, 1981]). My own previous work *Word and
   Supplement: Speech Acts, Biblical Texts and the Sufficiency of Scripture* (Oxford:
   Oxford University Press, 2002) has also been chided by a few for relying
   too heavily on a concept drawn from the philosophy of language,
   namely speech-act theory. I did not, though, mean to claim that the
   philosophy of language alone can provide the entire basis for a fully
   reworked doctrine of Scripture. I was using it as a tool to provide a fresh
   angle on Scripture, which future biblical and theological work might
   exploit. This book is an attempt at this latter task.

evangelical doctrine of Scripture in recent centuries, and because of criticisms regularly made of it.

Much evangelical writing on Scripture from the last four centuries has been taken to task for allegedly not being as truly theological as it should have been. That is, it is said that the doctrine of Scripture has not been integrally related to the primary Christian doctrines: the doctrines of God, Christ, the Spirit, creation and salvation. Indeed it is certainly the case that in the period following the Protestant Reformation in the sixteenth century a significant shift took place in the form in which evangelical theology was constructed. The sixteenth-century Reformers mostly did not devote an entire separate section to Scripture itself in their theological writings. Thus John Calvin's *Institutes of the Christian Religion* (1559) does not contain a section explicitly on Scripture. Instead he deals with Scripture within a more general opening section entitled 'The Knowledge of God the Creator'. By contrast, theologians of the following seventeenth century more usually opened their systematic theologies with an introductory discussion of the nature of theology itself (usually termed the 'prolegomena'), followed immediately by a section devoted entirely to the doctrine of Scripture. Only after this came discussions of God, creation, Christ and salvation. Modern works of evangelical systematic theology often follow this same pattern.

It is often said that this represents a major theological shift, and a mistaken one, in orthodox Protestant theology after the Reformation. The claim being made is that from the seventeenth century a doctrine of Scripture was developed as central to theology expressed in mostly philosophical and speculative terms, in isolation from the Bible's teaching about God and Christ. Thus the theology of the generations who came after the Reformers often stands accused of talking about the Bible without always being conscious, or at least making explicit, that we ought not to theologize and theorize about Scripture without beginning squarely with the Bible's teaching about God's character and actions. However, this interpretation of theology in the seventeenth and eighteenth centuries has been subjected to searching and persuasive criticism. What was happening was that theologians were changing the *format* in which they wrote their theology, but without substantially moving away from the basic theological views of the Bible that Luther, Calvin and others had articulated.[5]

Nevertheless it is probably the case that, since the eighteenth century, this revised format in which evangelical systematic theology has been presented has had some unforeseen negative impact on popular evangelical thought. Many presentations of evangelical theology often begin by discussing Scripture, and discuss Scripture under doctrinal headings such as Scripture's sufficiency, clarity and authority. It is certainly not the case that these headings are misleading; later in this book I shall defend them and explain them. The problem is, rather, that when the doctrine of Scripture is presented primarily in this form it can at least *appear* as if Scripture is unrelated to the great central doctrines of the Christian faith. At the very least, much contemporary evangelical teaching and writing on Scripture has not gone out of its way to demonstrate in its very content and form that such accusations are mistaken. The result can be that believers are left at least slightly unclear on just why the Bible ought to be so central to

---

5. See Carl R. Trueman and R. S. Clark (eds.), *Protestant Scholasticism: Essays in Reassessment* (Carlisle: Paternoster, 1999). On respectively Reformed and Lutheran theology of the post-Reformation period, see Richard A. Muller, *Post-Reformation Reformed Dogmatics*, vol. 2, *Holy Scripture: The Cognitive Foundation of Theology* (Grand Rapids: Baker, 1993); Robert D. Preus, *The Theology of Post-Reformation Lutheranism: A Study of Theological Prolegomena* (St. Louis: Concordia, 1970). The format of theology was changing in the seventeenth century because of the need to answer the increasingly sophisticated objections to the Reformation's view of the Bible, coming from both Roman Catholics and sceptics. Philosophical influences in the surrounding culture also affected the mode in which it was felt that theological arguments ought to be presented. Indeed the prolegomena of seventeenth-century systematic theologies, while addressing philosophical issues and drawing on philosophical concepts, are usually at root thoroughly biblical-theological in content. Thus the subsequent section on the doctrine of Scripture, when it comes, has been introduced theologically, even though the fuller discussions of God, Christ, Spirit and salvation come only later.

faith, and especially on how it can be kept central without itself attracting attention away from Christ, thereby becoming an idolatrous focus of worship.

Indeed if we talk about the Bible without explicitly structuring what we say about it around the great doctrines of God, Christ and the Spirit, then two unfortunate things happen. First, the doctrine of Scripture can begin to look like a preface or appendix to the central doctrines of the Christian faith, as these have been expressed in the church's great creeds. As such it can seem easily dispensable. (Most books, after all, lose very little of substance if stripped of their preface and appendices.) The doctrine of Scripture is certainly *not* dispensable, but evangelicals can sometimes, quite contrary to their intentions, make it appear so. This is an especially attractive option to anyone who has personal and painful experience of controversy between evangelicals over the nature of Scripture, and who has consequently come to think that focusing in doctrinal detail on Scripture usually results in a destructive fall away from Christ. It is also attractive to those Christians who wish to remain largely orthodox in their understanding of God, but who disagree with the orthodox doctrine of Scripture.

A second unfortunate consequence of a doctrine of Scripture developed apparently in isolation from other central Christian teachings, and from the shape of the narrative structure of Scripture as a whole, is that it can turn out to be a doctrine that seems impoverished and thin, lacking deep roots in the rich glories of the character and actions of God himself. This can be the case even if the doctrine, considered detail by detail, is unimpeachably orthodox and biblical. Such a doctrine can feel, even to some of those who at heart want to uphold it, more like an interesting and necessary tangent in theology than part of the heartbeat of theology itself. It comes to look like a kind of theological throat-clearing, prior to the main business of actually talking about God, as if in articulating the doctrine of Scripture we were really saying little more than this: 'Let's establish the basis on which we talk about God . . . and that's where the Bible comes in. Now that this is clear, we can get on with the business of actually talking about God.'

There may be times in Christian history when it is right to begin one's theology with the doctrine of Scripture, because the prevailing culture makes it important apologetically to address questions of how God can be known right at the outset. However, the doctrine of Scripture itself is often distorted through this approach, and therefore the kind of doctrine of Scripture this book will outline is one that aims to demonstrate that its every aspect is shaped from the bottom up by the character and actions of God, and is integrally related to God's being and action, yet without the inert book coming to eclipse the living Saviour.

After these biblical and theological outlines comes, thirdly, a *doctrinal outline* of Scripture. It is in this chapter that I discuss Scripture under the headings with which evangelicals are usually most familiar, namely Scripture's necessity, sufficiency, clarity and authority. These doctrinal headings certainly do flow naturally and necessarily out of the biblical and theological outlines of Scripture, and I shall be concerned to demonstrate carefully that that is the case. They are often termed the 'attributes' of Scripture, and the doctrinal outline will try to show that they are not a list of abstract qualities assigned to Scripture for questionable philosophical reasons. Instead they emerge as appropriate and necessary descriptions of Scripture, in the light of its dynamic and integral function within God's actions in the history of redemption. I shall offer a definition of each attribute, shaped by the preceding biblical and theological material.

The final major chapter seeks to open up some significant areas where the doctrine of Scripture, as I have outlined it, should be *applied*. We shall look first at that great slogan from the Reformation, *sola scriptura* (Scripture alone), and then more specifically at some basic questions about the place of Scripture within the Christian community. Then come two final sections: one on the nature of preaching, in the light of the nature and function of Scripture I am describing, and one on the appropriate role and aims of the private reading of Scripture by Christians. In these sections I want to demonstrate how a proper doctrine of Scripture can and should make the way a Christian approaches Scripture day by day more faithful, dynamic and life-giving.

To help the reader keep pace with the doctrine of Scripture which will build up as the book progresses, regular summary paragraphs have been included, often at the end of each major section.

It will be helpful to note here at the outset the theological writings on which I have drawn most heavily. As the book progresses, readers will find the names of certain theologians appearing more often than others in the text and footnotes. These are the four primary ones:

1. *John Calvin*, the great systematizer of Reformation theology in the sixteenth century.
2. *Francis Turretin* of Geneva, an influential and leading figure of Reformed theology from the middle of the seventeenth century.
3. *B. B. Warfield*, the American theologian of the late nineteenth and early twentieth centuries, whose writings on Scripture have set the agenda for many debates on Scripture in the last century, especially in the United States.
4. *Herman Bavinck*, Warfield's brilliant contemporary in Holland.

It is not that all four agree with each other on every detail; nor are they to be slavishly followed at every point, since like us they were fallible people. Nor am I suggesting that nothing worthwhile has been written on Scripture since the 1950s; the writings of J. I. Packer, for example, have helped many people understand and remain committed to the evangelical doctrine of Scripture in recent decades. Nevertheless in the works of these four older theologians we are given some of the great high points in Christian history of the explanation and defence of the evangelical doctrine of Scripture. We are therefore impoverished in coming to grips with Scripture in our own day, and dealing with contemporary challenges to Scripture, if we are not rooted in the thought of people such as these.

Overall, then, this book intends to describe the nature and function of Scripture in explicitly biblical and theological terms, as well as doctrinal ones. I aim to offer an outline of the doctrine of Scripture that stands firmly in line with the best of the theological traditions that have come down to us, and that is also expressed in a form appropriate for the twenty-first century. If it turns out that this will help some readers to understand God's actions in and through Scripture in a little more depth, and so worship the God of Scripture with greater assurance and joy, then my aims will have been fulfilled.

2. GOD AND SCRIPTURE: A BIBLICAL OUTLINE

The fundamental question to which we seek an answer in this chapter is: What, according to the Bible, is in fact going on when God speaks? We need to be clear on this, if what we eventually say about our understanding of the Bible as the 'Word of God' is going to be true and coherent. The focus will be on how God relates himself to words, both spoken and written. Therefore this chapter will sketch an outline of how central language is to who God and Christ are, and to what they do. If this way of putting it sounds a little abstract to some readers, the picture being pieced together here should become increasingly clear as the chapter progresses.

God's action and his words

The Old Testament
It is often observed that God's words and actions are intimately related in the Bible. To say of God that he spoke, and to say of God that he did something, is often one and the same thing. The

examples that follow here have been drawn deliberately from different parts of the Bible. One of the most obvious examples is found in the biblical creation accounts. According to the Bible, God creates by speaking: 'God said, "Let there be light," and there was light' (Gen. 1:3). It seems that here God expressing the wish that light exist, and the coming into existence of light, are two ways of describing the same event. In Genesis 1:6 he says, 'let there be a vault between the waters', and verse 7 adds, 'so God made the vault'. In the light of verse 3, verses 6 and 7 do not appear to be describing two different actions. It is not the case that God first expresses verbally his desire to create and then actually forms creation wordlessly. A more natural reading is that verses 6 and 7 give two different aspects of the single divine act of creation. The rest of Genesis chapter 1 follows the same pattern. In some cases God's act of speaking is simply sufficient for an act of creation, with no additional account of God 'making' or 'creating' (as in vv. 9 and 11, each of which ends with the simple description 'and it was so'). In others his creative words are followed by a summary description of what that act of speech has achieved ('God made/created . . .', vv. 14–16, 20–21, 24–25, 26–27).

Immediately after the creation comes the account of the fall, where humankind sins and, along with the rest of the world, comes under God's curse. Following humanity's creation by means of an act of speech, it is tragically fitting that humanity's fall should also be precipitated partly by language. For that is indeed how it happens. The snake mounts his attack on humanity, and therefore on God's action in creation, by speaking. He speaks words that call into question the reality of what God had in fact commanded. God had said, 'You must not eat from the tree of the knowledge of good and evil, for when you eat of it you will certainly die' (Gen. 2:17). The snake throws this clear command into confusion first by distorting God's words, 'Did God really say, "You must not eat from *any* tree in the garden"?' (Gen. 3:1), and then by explicitly denying the fatal consequence God declared would follow from disobedience to his command: 'You will not certainly die' (Gen. 3:4).

God's immediate response to these tragic events is to speak directly himself. He first calls to the man, 'Where are you?' (Gen.

3:9), and then proceeds to pronounce curses on the serpent, on the woman and on the ground, and by extension on the man (Gen. 3:14–19). It would have been quite possible for God to have introduced painful child-bearing into the woman's life, and to have made the snake crawl on its belly, and made the man's labour on the land difficult, all without speaking, by wordless acts of judgment. However, the God who is presented to us in the Bible is quite unlike that: he is a God who, by his very nature, acts by speaking. The divine word that created in the first place continues to speak in warning humanity against disobedience to God, and subsequently in uttering curses when disobedience occurs. And the act of cursing is for God as effective as the act of creating; for God to say the words is to perform the action.

God's speaking activity in the Old Testament continues, as his plan of redemption begins to unfold. This redemption was first hinted at even in the pronouncing of the curse back in the fall (Gen. 3:15). As Scripture develops, it becomes clear that the primary form in which God works for the redemption of humanity from the curse of sin and death is *through his establishment of the covenant*. A covenant, of course, is at heart a relationship established by means of the uttering of a promise.[1] Thus the covenant with Noah, symbolized by the rainbow, takes the form of a spoken promise never again to destroy the earth by a flood (Gen. 9:8–17). This is God, as throughout the Old Testament, tying his future actions to the words of his promise.

The same is evident a few chapters further on in Genesis, when God begins the long redemptive process of forming a people who will bear his name, through the calling of Abraham (as Abram). Again, we could imagine the possibility of God beginning this long historical process through silent acts in history, providentially prompting Abraham to move from his homeland to the land that

---

1. Telford Work has a helpful description of the place of God's words in the redemption history of Israel in *Living and Active: Scripture in the Economy of Salvation* (Grand Rapids: Eerdmans, 2002), pp. 130–166. For example, 'a fundamental part of God's mercy to Israel certainly took the form of words' (p. 136).

God intended for him. Instead, though, God acts by speaking. He calls Abraham, and makes a covenant promise, which Abraham is invited to accept as his solid basis for trusting that God will do what he undertakes to do (Gen. 12:1–3). In giving Abraham the words of a promise ('all peoples on earth will be blessed through you') God commits himself to a course of faithful action that leads up to the birth of Christ and the pouring out of the Spirit at Pentecost, and continues through the present 'last days' right up until the future return of Christ. With these words God defines and explains the goal of his future redemptive activity, committing himself to a particular course of action in history.

It is helpful to show that the point being illustrated here (that God in the Bible very often acts simply by speaking) is not an event that occurs only at the high points of God's linguistic action, such as his creating, cursing, and covenant-making. Instead it is a characteristic of God's action that runs throughout the Old Testament. The following examples, from different literary genres within the Old Testament, are chosen almost at random to demonstrate this point.

The same relationship between God's action and his words can be found, for example, in 1 Kings 13. This chapter recounts at some length the strange and sad events that took place immediately after the division of Israel into two kingdoms, north and south, which occurred under Jeroboam. A prophet came from Judah to Israel, but was deceived into disobeying the words God had already spoken to him. Thus the chapter begins, 'By the word of the LORD a man of God came from Judah to Bethel, as Jeroboam was standing by the altar to make an offering. He cried out against the altar by the word of the LORD, "Altar, altar! This is what the LORD says . . ."' (vv. 1–2). The key phrase '[by] the word of the LORD' becomes the great refrain of the chapter (vv. 5, 9, 20, 21, 26, 32), such that the 'word' emerges as the main agent in driving the narrative forward. One commentator judges that 'This is a story about the word's power to get itself done.'[2] Words on their own, though, can of course get

---

2. Richard Nelson, *1 & 2 Kings*, Interpretation Commentary (Louisville: John Knox, 1987), pp. 84–85.

nothing done. The word of the Lord has power only because it is the Lord who sends it. Therefore ascribing to 'the word' the ability to perform certain actions, turning the word itself into an agent, is a way of talking about God himself performing certain actions. For 1 Kings 13 to say that an event happened 'by the word of the LORD' is synonymous with saying 'God acted by means of language in order to cause it to happen'.

The same equation of God speaking and God acting is evident in Psalm 29. A central theme of this psalm is the power of God's voice:

> The voice of the LORD breaks the cedars;
>   the LORD breaks in pieces the cedars of Lebanon . . .
> The voice of the LORD shakes the desert;
>   the LORD shakes the Desert of Kadesh.
> (Ps. 29:5, 8)

The poetic parallelism of each of these verses equates God performing an action by means of his voice, with God simply performing that action himself. Each half of each verse is a different way of talking about the same divine reality. Therefore to say of God that he did something, and to say that his voice did something, is to refer to the same action of God in two different ways.

A classic passage in this regard is Isaiah 55:10–11:

> As the rain and the snow
>   come down from heaven,
> and do not return to it
>   without watering the earth
> and making it bud and flourish,
>   so that it yields seed for the sower and bread for the eater,
> so is my word that goes out from my mouth:
>   it will not return to me empty,
> but will accomplish what I desire
>   and achieve the purpose for which I sent it.

The transcendent God here describes his word as the means by which he acts in the world. The language about God's 'word' seems to be a way of speaking of God's active presence in the world. This avoids such a strong insistence on transcendence as God's primary mode of being that his presence in the world comes to seem bizarre or incomprehensible, while also steering away from a collapse into a view of God as primarily or exclusively immanent. God and his word share the divine ability infallibly to perform their purpose; human words often fail to perform their intended purpose, but God's words do not. Thus an action of God can be appropriately described both by saying that God's Word has performed an action for which he sent it, and by saying that God himself has performed an action.

The New Testament

Moving to the New Testament, the relationship between Christ's words and the action of God will be outlined later in this chapter. However, at this point two examples from the New Testament's teaching on God's action in salvation can be given. First, orthodox Protestant theology has regularly identified an aspect of the divine act of salvation in which God *declares* the sinner to be righteous in his sight. This point has traditionally been developed under the heading of 'justification', with the aim of making clear that God restores us into proper relationship with himself prior to, rather than subsequent to or simultaneous with, any actual change in our spiritual state. As the apostle Paul says, 'While we were still sinners, Christ died for us' (Rom. 5:8). God establishes, by his own declaration, a fundamental change in our standing before him, before he brings about, by the sending of the Holy Spirit, a real change to our sinful state. There is a clear parallel here with the accounts in Genesis of God's acts of creation discussed above. God did not declare his intention to make us holy before him, and then get on and make us fit to enter a relationship with him. Instead he spoke, making us by that declaration to be justified in our relationship with him. Then he subsequently went on to bring about in our lives, by an increase in holiness, the necessary and natural effects of that change in our standing before him. This wonderful reality in the practice of God's work of salvation is illustrated in the willingness of Jesus to talk and share food with social outcasts and notorious sinners, often to the horror of the religious establishment. Thus a fundamental aspect of God's redemptive work occurs when he chooses to speak, and in so doing unilaterally brings us to share here and now in the right standing with him that Jesus Christ has.

Secondly, Protestant theology has often discerned in the New Testament's description of salvation an act of God that has been called his 'effectual calling'. This is an act of God by which he calls us to be saved, and where the very action of calling itself brings us to salvation (see e.g. Rom. 8:30). God can choose to call people to himself in such a way that it is appropriate to say that the call itself brings about in the person's heart the very thing God intends, namely that they respond in saving faith. In other words God speaks not just to *describe* salvation to us, or to encourage us to come to him to be saved, although he certainly does both these things. God *speaking* is also an integral part of God *acting* to save. Thus, in biblical language and theology, *God speaking and God acting are often one and the same thing.*

God's person and his words

Now we need to consider the relationship between God's person (God himself) and the words he speaks. What we find in Scripture is an astoundingly close relationship between God himself and the words through which he speaks.

This is evident as early as Eden. God has established a relationship between himself and Adam and Eve in part by means of a command ('you must not eat from the tree of the knowledge of good and evil') and a threatened consequence if the command is disobeyed ('for when you eat of it you will certainly die', Gen. 2:17). These words also imply a positive promise: the blessings of life in the garden will continue to flow to humanity if they obey God's command. Humanity's fall into sin is a fall into disobedience in this relationship which God has established between himself and his human creatures, and occurs when they disobey his verbal command. God's action in response is to curse, fulfilling the negative promise of Genesis 2:17 with a curse that amounts to a spiritual death, since it cuts humanity off from the tree of life

(Gen. 2:24), and that later climaxes in physical death (Gen. 5:5). Thus, when Adam and Eve disobey God's *spoken command*, they fracture their relationship with *God himself*. From God's side, when the words of his command are set aside by his creatures in favour of their own desires and their own claims of wisdom, then God himself has been set aside.

What this suggests about the relationship between God and his words seems rather obvious. To disobey the words God speaks is simply to disobey God himself, and to refuse to submit to the commands God utters is simply to break one's relationship with him. Thus (we may say) God has *invested* himself in his words, or we could say that God has so *identified* himself with his words that whatever someone does to God's words (whether it is to obey or to disobey) they do directly to God himself. Obvious though this may seem, in the following pages we shall discover that its implications are enormous. When they are overlooked, it is always detrimental to our understanding of Scripture. To ask how or why this can be, that words and persons can be so intimately related, is to enter deep theological and philosophical waters (into some of which we shall dip our toes in the next chapter). What does it *mean* for God to invest himself in his words, or to identify himself with his words? The complexities of this notwithstanding, the point itself is quite a straightforward one.

Although the word 'covenant' is not used in these opening chapters of Genesis, it has commonly been thought that God relates to Adam and Eve in a *covenantal* manner, that is, according to the same pattern he will repeat constantly in his ongoing relationships with his human creatures, and that will become the fundamental characteristic of his redemptive relationship with humanity. Common characteristics of God's covenant with his people are his declaration of the relationship he is establishing between himself and his people, his explanation of how his people must live as covenant partners, promises of blessings if they remain faithfully within the covenant, and warnings of disasters if they abandon their covenant responsibilities. In the case of Adam and Eve it is a covenant that implicitly promises life. In the case of Abraham it is a covenant that promises that blessing will come to all peoples on earth in some way 'through' Abraham (Gen. 12:3).

God comes to Abraham initially with a command: 'Go from
your country, your people and your father's household to the land I
will show you' (Gen. 12:1). The promise that God will make
Abraham into a great nation and bless all peoples on earth through
him follows on directly (vv. 2–3), and seems by implication to
depend on Abraham acting in faithful obedience to the command.
Here, at the birth of God's covenant people, God relates himself
to his people by speaking. Abraham leaves his home in Haran and
sets out. He does so in direct obedience to God's command, and
trusting that God will keep the promises he has made. Merely in so
doing, obeying the words of command and trusting the words of
a promise, Abraham enters into a covenant relationship with God.
In other words Abraham's response to God's words simply is also
a response to God himself. His obedience to and trust in God's
words are also, at one and the same time, an obedience to and trust
in God himself. Thus in straightforward and apparently unsophis-
ticated ways Scripture reveals profound things about God's
relationship to the words he speaks.

The same feature underlies the next manifestation of the
covenant, which is the covenant of law proclaimed by God
through Moses. It is prefaced with a repetition by God to Moses
of the promise regarding the land which God had made to
Abraham and his descendants ('I will bring you to the land I
swore with uplifted hand to give to Abraham, to Isaac and to
Jacob. I will give it to you as a possession. I am the LORD', Exod.
6:8). This demonstrates that this covenant is a further revelation
of the covenant initiated with Abraham, not a replacement for it.
It is then inaugurated with these words at Sinai, spoken by God
to Moses on the mountain, and to be passed on to the whole
nation of Israel:

> This is what you are to say to the house of Jacob and what you are to tell
> the people of Israel: 'You yourselves have seen what I did to Egypt, and
> how I carried you on eagles' wings and brought you to myself. Now if
> you obey me fully and keep my covenant, then out of all nations you will
> be my treasured possession. Although the whole earth is mine, you will
> be for me a kingdom of priests and a holy nation.' These are the words
> you are to speak to the Israelites. (Exod. 19:3b–6)

Once redeemed by this gracious and sovereign act of God in the exodus, God's people continue to relate to him as their God by obeying the stipulations of a verbal covenant. They will retain the identity and status they have by virtue of the relationship God is developing with them ('a kingdom of priests and a holy nation') only if they remain faithful to the new words God will speak to them. Thus the reality and nature of their relationship with God himself will be determined entirely by the reality and nature of their relationship to the *words* God is about to speak to them.

This point is dramatically illustrated for the covenant people in the establishment of the tabernacle, whose physical features are prescribed in extraordinary detail in the Mosaic covenant (Exod. 25 – 30). At the heart of the tabernacle (and then subsequently at the heart of the more permanent temple in Jerusalem) sat the ark of the covenant, containing the stones inscribed with the summary of the covenant law (Exod. 25:10–22). Moreover it was directly over this ark, containing God's covenant words, that God promised to meet with Moses and speak to him (Exod. 25:22). This was a powerful illustration of all God's covenant-based relationships with his people. His words, literally written in stone, represented the place where he met with the leader of his people, at the centre of their encampment (and later at the centre of their city, Jerusalem). This spoke powerfully of the fact that God's words were in some sense the mode in which he had chosen to be present among his people.

It also explains why people are regarded as having acted directly in relation to God simply by acting in relation to the inanimate ark of the covenant, experiencing sometimes blessing and sometimes judgment as a result (as is especially narrated in 2 Sam. 6, where the Lord's anger burns against someone who touches the ark irreverently, and his blessing falls on a household in which the ark is placed). The point is not that God has 'reached down' to invest an inanimate object with a reflection of his divine powers, such that the ark or the tablets *as objects in their own right* have the power to bring blessing or judgment; this is not a question of magical 'holy' objects. Nor is it the case that God establishes an arbitrary test 'from above' in relation to the ark, as if he were saying, 'Touch it irreverently and bad things will happen; bring it respectfully into your house and I'll bless you. That's just the way I've chosen to operate.' Instead God has in reality so linked himself with the words inscribed on the tablets in the ark that he is, in some sense, present in those words. Telford Work has explored this point well in the Old Testament: 'It is *in* the Ark of God and *in* the words said to reside there that ancient Israel sees God savingly present.'[3]

The nature of the 'personal presence' represented by a person's written words is something to be explored in the next chapter. For now, though, as throughout this chapter, we simply note that Scripture makes the point quite clearly that God's words in some way convey his presence.

We now need to pause and take stock a little. The covenantal nature of God's relationship with his people should lead us to draw two conclusions about God's own relationship to the words he speaks. First, it is in and through *the words of the covenant* he speaks to his people that God makes himself knowable to humanity. We come to know other people by living for a time in relationship with them, listening to them speak about themselves and others, and watching them act. Here in the Old Testament covenant, God graciously allows his people to come to know him in the same way. Of course it is not that God speaks only but does not act, since his prime act in the Pentateuch is the redemption of his people from Egypt through the exodus. However, as has often been pointed out, the exodus as an event would be incomprehensible as divine redemption to those experiencing it, were it not preceded and followed by explanatory words from God. Moreover, God decreed that the exodus event should set a pattern (a typological pattern) for the entirety of his redemptive work, and that the memory of the event should shape the life of his people for the future, by means of verbal repetition of the event and its meaning (Exod. 12:24–28).

Thus God identifies himself for his people as the God of Abraham, Isaac and Jacob: the God who makes and keeps his covenant with his people. God promises us that he really is the God

---

3. Work, *Living and Active*, p. 142 (italics original).

who presents himself to us in the covenant he establishes between himself and us. The covenant is not a means by which God deals with us, as it were, at arm's length. God's covenant is not a form of mediation, transaction or negotiation that takes place between essentially separate persons, with God remaining entirely transcendent. It is not a relationship where God himself remains fundamentally absent. Rather the covenant, and therefore the human words in which the covenant is given expression and enacted, are the means by which God elects to be God in relationship with us. It is the very means by which he comes to be God for us. Thus when Abram hears and obeys the divine command to leave Haran and go to the land the Lord will show him, he thereby comes directly into relationship with God. To trust God's covenant promise is not to enter into an agreement with an absentee God; it is to trust the God who has come to you. There is, then, a complex but real relationship between God and his actions, expressed and performed, as they are, through God's words. In philosophical terms, there is an ontological relationship between God and his words. It seems that *God's actions, including his verbal actions, are a kind of extension of him.*

Our second reflection about the covenant is this: God cannot meaningfully establish his covenant with us, he cannot make his promise to us, without using words. God's covenant promise is a complicated affair, in which God is referring to himself, to the relationship he is establishing between himself and his people, to what is now required of his people, and also referring to the future, promising a future of blessing if his people keep the covenant, and warning of a cursed future if they disobey. None of this is possible without words. God chooses to use words as a fundamental means of relating to us, we must presume, because the kind of relationship he chooses to establish cannot be established without them. Moreover, the words he uses need to be words human beings can comprehend, since only if the covenant promise is given in such words is it a covenant to which we can respond.

All of this means that words, including human words, do not necessarily obscure a relationship with God, somehow getting in the way. More mystically minded people sometimes suppose that words by their very nature are an obstruction to the goal of a deep communion with God, but that is just not so. Instead words are a necessary medium of a relationship with God. To put your trust in the words of the covenant promise God makes to you is itself to put your trust in God: the two are the same thing. *Communication from* God is therefore *communion with* God, when met with a response of trust from us.

This is not to say that words are everything, as if speaking and being spoken to constitute the whole of our relationship with God. The kingdom of God is not just a matter of talk. There are and should be varieties of wordless contemplation of God, and wordless resting in his presence. Yet it remains true that, if the God with whom we are in relationship is to be the true God and not an idol, our only access to a real relationship with the living God in which words sometimes fall away is precisely in and through words which God speaks to us. After all, a man and a woman sitting in a restaurant gazing silently into each other's eyes over the table are engaging in a much more genuine relationship if they are doing so with twenty years of conversation-filled marriage behind them, than if they are on their first date and have not yet spoken to each other.

It is of course a dangerous mistake to suppose that the words by which God chooses to establish his relationship with us present him to us exhaustively. There is much that we do not know about God and his actions, simply because God has not told us. In Christian living and thinking there is a right place for the mystery of God, as the Lord states forcefully to Job (Job 38 – 41). However, a necessary focus on God as mystery must not be allowed to obscure the extraordinary act of grace by which God speaks to us human words of promise, such that for us to trust those words is in itself an act of trusting God himself.

God's words and human words

The third relationship to consider is that between God's words and human words. With a great deal of God's speech in Scripture, especially in the Old Testament, the precise way God 'speaks' is not made known to us. Many Bible readers ask at this point, 'What does it really mean to say that God "speaks", when he has no physical vocal cords with which to make sounds, and no physical hand with which to write?' In the face of this question some, it is true, have concluded that we ought to stop saying of God that he 'speaks', and instead speak of him as prompting, guiding and overseeing, or using some other similar wordless actions. However, a little thought about 'speech' even between human beings shows that we need not jump to that conclusion. We can 'speak' through movements of our hands in sign language, or through flashes of light from one ship to another in Morse code, or through a message delivered on our behalf by another (such as an ambassador communicating a message from one head of state to another). Thus the notion of 'speaking' can be extended beyond face-to-face and speaker-to-hearer contact, and even beyond the movement of air over vocal cords or of a pen over paper, while still being identifiably and meaningfully 'speech'.

Now if we carry this thought over to what is meant by God's speech, we find ourselves asking: exactly what was happening when God 'spoke' and 'called' in the garden to Adam and Eve, when he 'spoke' to Abraham, commanding him to leave home and making great promises to him, and when he 'spoke' to Moses on the top of the mountain, giving him the covenant law to be delivered to the whole of Israel? We may speculate about this, but the true answer is that we cannot be sure, because we are not told. However, the diversity of forms of 'speech' even among human beings, which go far beyond actual utterances by lips, means that God's incorporeal nature cannot be said to render him incapable of speech.[4]

As the Old Testament unfolds, one form of divine speaking does emerge as prominent: God's speech through his appointed

---

4. For further reflection on this, see Nicholas Wolterstorff, *Divine Discourse: Philosophical Reflections on the Claim that God Speaks* (Cambridge: Cambridge University Press, 1995); Michael S. Horton, *Covenant and Eschatology: The Divine Drama* (Louisville: Westminster John Knox, 2002).

prophets, in words they utter in ordinary human languages. The Old Testament regularly assumes that God can and does speak in and through certain human words, in such a way that those words can truly be said to be his words. This is remarkable, but is so common in Scripture that most people familiar with the Bible have ceased to be astounded by it. The Bible gives no worked-through theological or philosophical account of how human words can be said to be also words from God. Indeed for many people this claim has seemed absurd, and even idolatrous. How can something as limited as human language ever be said to convey anything of God reliably?

The Bible hints at its answer to this in its account of the creation of humanity. God makes his human creatures, as he says, 'in our image, in our likeness' (Gen. 1:26). The precise meaning of this phrase is of course much discussed, but it must be significant that, in the immediate context of Genesis 1, the activity of God referred to most frequently is his speaking. In this light it seems that 'the image of God' in humanity must include at least some reference to humanity's capacity for complex language, as a reflection of God's own character as a speaking God. Indeed God's use of a first-person plural pronoun in the creation of humanity ('let us make . . .'), following directly on from his acts of speaking earlier in the chapter, may be best understood as an early hint of what the New Testament will reveal to be a plurality of communicating persons within 'God'.[5] Whatever else may be true of human language, it is quite reasonable to suppose that it has the ability to speak truly of God, both because it was given to us by a God who speaks within himself as eternally three speaking persons, and also because our possession of language, as made in God's image, is analogous to God's communicative capacity. Our language can be made by God to speak truthfully of him because our language has

---

5. I know this interpretation of Gen. 1:26 is unfashionable, but it seems to me a more likely explanation than the idea that God is addressing the 'royal court' of the heavenly host, or that he is using some divine version of the 'royal we', as favoured by some powerful humans. It is more likely because it is related to God's repeated activity throughout the chapter.

its origin in him and in some way is like his own. The fall makes this much more problematic, of course, but sin does not erase humanity as the image of God, and thus does not destroy the capacity of human language to speak truly of God.

Throughout the life of Moses, in particular, God gives him words to speak to the rest of the people of Israel that, although delivered by a man in ordinary language, are to be identified as also God's words. This general principle of prophetic speech is expressed powerfully in Deuteronomy 18:15–20, where God promises to send a prophet after Moses: 'I will put my words in his mouth' (v. 18). The opening of the book of Jeremiah provides an excellent example of the complete identification of the prophet's words with God's words. God says to Jeremiah, 'I have put my words in your mouth. See, today I appoint you over nations and kingdoms to uproot and tear down, to destroy and overthrow, to build and to plant' (Jer. 1:9b–10). Jeremiah is appointed by God to have power over nations and kingdoms, but this power comes only from the divine words God has put in his mouth. Only God has this power over nations. Jeremiah, as his deputized speaker, is given the same power only in that he speaks words given him by God – words which therefore can perform what God intends them to perform. Jeremiah will speak ordinary human words in an ordinary human language; God does not put special magic formulae or a previously unknown heavenly language into Jeremiah's mouth. Yet still those words will also be God's words. Jeremiah's words are ordinary human words, but are not any less divine for also being fully human. In a rather different incident, God put his words into the mouth of Balaam, and even into the mouth of his donkey (Num. 22). In so doing the Lord was perhaps warning Israelite prophets not to get too presumptuous or arrogant, just because the Lord sometimes used them to speak his words.

This identification of human and divine words extends beyond actual prophetic speech and also covers written texts, within the Old Testament itself. This point has been argued recently with regard to the book of Jeremiah by Gordon McConville. He points out how Jeremiah 36 allows for the word once given to the prophet to be written down and to be effective as God's speech beyond Jeremiah's life and beyond the circumstances in which the word was first given to him.[6] This is so because that chapter tells how Jeremiah dictated to a scribe all the words God had delivered to him, and the scribe wrote them on a scroll designed for public proclamation. As regards the non-prophetic aspects of the book, McConville argues that the experiences of Jeremiah which the book narrates, whose suffering reflects God's suffering over Israel's unfaithfulness, 'all in some sense mark the involvement of God in Israel's history, in a way that may be called "incarnational"'. In adding both this theme and the clear hope of a new covenant to the wider Old Testament canon, the book of Jeremiah as a whole becomes part of God's speaking through Scripture.[7] The non-prophetic, prosaic parts of the book are therefore woven intricately together with actual prophetic speech in a form that subsequent communities received in its entirety as canonical.[8]

It is probably helpful *to summarize the biblical outline of this chapter so far.* When we encounter certain *human words* (e.g. the words of an Old Testament prophet), we are in direct contact with *God's words.* This is itself a direct encounter with *God's activity* (since God's speech is one form in which he regularly acts), especially with his *covenant-making* activity. And an encounter with God's covenant-making communicative activity is *itself an encounter with God.*

So far the main focus has been on the Old Testament. We turn now to the New Testament, to consider the relationship of the words spoken by Jesus Christ, the Word incarnate, to God's action and person.

----

6. Gordon McConville, 'Divine Speech and the Book of Jeremiah', in Paul Helm and Carl Trueman (eds.), *The Trustworthiness of God: Perspectives on the Nature of Scripture* (Leicester: Apollos, 2002), pp. 25–26.

7. Ibid., pp. 32, 37.

8. Herman Bavinck says, 'word and fact, the religious and the historical dimensions, that which was spoken by God and that which was spoken by human beings, is [*sic*] so tightly interwoven and intertwined that separation is impossible. The historical parts in Scripture are also a revelation of God' (Herman Bavinck, *Reformed Dogmatics*, vol. 1, *Prolegomena*, gen. ed. John Bolt, tr. John Vriend [Grand Rapids: Baker Academic, 2003], p. 438).

9-11

Christ's words, and God's action and person

Jesus Christ comes as the fulfilment of all the Old Testament's covenant promises. In particular, as the Word-made-flesh he comes as the fulfilment of everything 'the word of God' in the Old Testament had been anticipating.

Although this is made clear throughout the New Testament, it is especially evident in the writings of John. Jesus says to one of his disciples, in John's Gospel, as something of a summary of this point, 'Don't you know me, Philip, even after I have been among you such a long time? Anyone who has seen me has seen the Father' (John 14:9). He is claiming that anyone who has encountered him in person has, in so doing, encountered God. As the early church soon came to realize, it was not just that Christ's words and actions were a much clearer reflection of the image of God in a human being than could be found in anyone else. Much more than that, to encounter Christ was in itself to encounter God, albeit in the hitherto unexpected form of a human individual. Elsewhere in the New Testament, Paul is claiming precisely the same thing when he refers to Christ as 'the power of God and the wisdom of God' (1 Cor. 1:24), and as the one in whom 'God was pleased to have all his fullness dwell' (Col. 1:19). It is worth noting, incidentally, that comments such as these by Paul demonstrate that this view of Christ was a feature not just of John's writing in the New Testament, but was also central to the apostolic proclamation of Christ from the beginning.

This 'fullness' of God in Christ includes of course Christ's *actions*. Jesus goes on to explain to Philip, in the passage from John just quoted, 'it is the Father, living in me, who is doing his work. Believe me when I say that I am in the Father and the Father is in me' (John 14:10b–11a). Earlier in the Gospel he has said something similar: 'Very truly I tell you, the Son can do nothing by himself; he can do only what he sees his Father doing, because whatever the Father does the Son also does' (5:19). Therefore to witness (e.g.) the Son raise Lazarus from the dead was directly to witness God's power over death at work. And the people who were healed of sickness by a word or touch from Christ were directly healed by the restoring action of God.

Moreover, the 'fullness' of God, which God was pleased to have dwell in Christ, also included the *words* Christ spoke. It is important to linger over this point for a moment. Christ says, 'I do nothing on my own but speak just what the Father has taught me' (John 8:28b). Also, 'I did not speak on my own, but the Father who sent me commanded me to say all that I have spoken. I know that his command leads to eternal life. So whatever I say is just what the Father has told me to say' (John 12:49–50). And again, praying to his Father about his disciples, Jesus says, 'I gave them the words you gave me' (John 17:8a). The most likely implication is that these words were given by the Father to Christ in eternity, and not exclusively during his earthly life, such as during his childhood, or his adult life before the beginning of his public ministry, or during the forty days in the wilderness, or throughout his life (say, during times of prayer), although none of these can be entirely ruled out. This becomes clearer if we continue reading the last verse quoted (John 17:8): 'They [the disciples] knew with certainty that I came from you, and they believed that you sent me.' Although this statement on its own is inconclusive proof of Christ's pre-existence (for that, a more wide-ranging case needs to be made, and can be made, from the New Testament as a whole), the strong implication is that the Father gave the Son the words he would speak on earth *before* his 'coming' and his 'being sent' by the Father.

We can say, then, that these statements by Jesus provide a glimpse into the eternal life of the triune God. It is a glimpse of the Father preparing for the appearing of the Son in human form by giving him words he would speak during his earthly ministry. The humble obedience of the Son is therefore seen not just in his painful and willing submission to suffering and death, but also in his faithful and obedient passing on of words he had been taught by his Father. As result, his earthly existence in its entirety, in both deed *and* word, was a genuine revelation of the wisdom and power of God. If this is right, then the statements from Jesus we have just been considering constitute a fuller revelation of the communicative activity that exists between the persons of the Trinity, first hinted at in the accounts in Genesis 1 of the creation of the universe and of humanity.

This sheds light on what Jesus means when he says, 'The words I have spoken to you – they are full of the Spirit and life' (John 6:63). It is not that Jesus is saying in some metaphorical sense that his words will bring fullness of life and lead people to walk in the power of the Spirit, if they obey them, true though that may be. Instead he means what he (literally) says: because his words are words which God identifies as entirely his own, they are literally 'full of the Spirit', who is himself God, and full of eternal life. For how could words that have their origin in God and that God names as his own be anything else?

In the same passage, where many of Christ's followers are deserting him, he asks Peter, 'You do not want to leave too, do you?' Peter replies, 'Lord, to whom shall we go? You have the words of eternal life. We have come to believe and to know that you are the Holy One of God' (John 6:67–69). At this early stage in the development of the disciples' understanding of Christ it is hard to be certain precisely what Peter is asserting here. At the time it may well have been simply a forceful way of saying something like 'As the Messiah, you faithfully speak the messianic message that God has given you.' However that may be, subsequent reflection by the apostles on Christ's life and teaching quickly led to the much stronger claim I have been outlining here: the straightforward but extraordinary claim that God the Son, the Word incarnate, speaks to us in ordinary human words the very things he has heard God the Father say within the eternal life of the Trinity. John begins his first letter by making precisely this point:

> That which was from the beginning, which we have heard, which we have seen with our eyes, which we have looked at and our hands have touched – this we proclaim concerning the Word of life. The life appeared; we have seen it and testify to it, and we proclaim to you the eternal life, which was with the Father and has appeared to us. (1 John 1:1–2)

That which was with the Father and has now been revealed in Christ (what John here calls 'the Word of life . . . the eternal life') includes, as he describes it, both Christ's actions *and* his words.

Christ's words and human words

Jesus' earthly ministry was limited in time and space. The Word
was made flesh in one individual, to live one actual human life and
to die one death. This is often described as the 'scandal of particularity', and throughout history many who have been presented
with the gospel of Christ have stumbled over it. Many Greeks who
heard the apostles proclaiming Christ as the risen Lord and as the
coming judge were not open to the possibility of God's truth
being revealed in the life of one individual born in a Palestinian
backwater. They expected to find it instead in a 'wisdom' that
would seem to them more obviously to be of divine origin. Paul
responds to this in 1 Corinthians 2:20–25 in his defence of his
preaching of the cross.

In a similar vein, some sixteen centuries later, many post-
Enlightenment Protestant theologians were happy to continue to
talk about the divine origin of Scripture, as long as Scripture could
be stripped of its historical particularities, in order to reveal a set
of supposedly universal moral and human truths. A key figure in
the development of this approach to Scripture was Baruch
Spinoza, a seventeenth-century Dutch thinker. For Spinoza the
history and doctrine the Bible contains are of no authority for us;
religion and biblical authority are matters of *morality* alone. What
he says of the prophets is representative of his attitude to the
whole Bible: 'the authority of the prophets has weight only in
matters of morality, and . . . their speculative doctrines affect us
little'.[9] The philosophical conviction underlying this view of the
Bible is summed up in the often-quoted assertion of the
eighteenth-century German writer G. E. Lessing, that 'accidental
truths of history can never become the proof of necessary truths
of reason'.[10]

---

9. Spinoza, *Tractatus Theologico-Politicus*, in *The Chief Works of Benedict de
   Spinoza*, vol. 1, tr. R. H. M. Elwes (London: George Bell & Sons, 1883),
   p. 8.
10. Lessing, *Lessing's Theological Writings*, ed. Henry Chadwick (London: A. &
    C. Black, 1956), p. 53.

This philosophical assertion continues, sometimes unconsciously and therefore unquestioned, to shape much contemporary rejection of the orthodox doctrine of Scripture. At root, the rejection of Scripture as divine special revelation is often a side effect of the greater rejection of the particularity of Christ as God's ultimate self-revelation in the world. Here should be noted a feature that underlies many discussions about Scripture: people's view of Scripture is often largely determined by their view of Jesus Christ. That is one practical reason why the doctrine of Scripture must be articulated in a way that makes explicit its dependence on the doctrine of Christ.

Of course, the particularity of revelation in Christ leads directly to a universal offer of new life in him. The Old Testament is the story both of the expansion of God's people, and also of the narrowing of God's redemptive purposes, as the southern kingdom of Judah stays centre stage while the northern kingdom of Israel disappears; as the 'faithful remnant' emerges as more significant in God's purposes for salvation than the nation as a whole; and as Israel's hopes for the future become focused on the emergence of a single Messiah figure. This narrowing reaches a climax with the arrival of Christ. He is the new Moses proclaiming a new law, and the new David establishing God's reign on earth. Yet he is also representative of the nation of Israel as a whole, tempted by Satan in the desert, just as they were. And he is representative of the whole of the new humanity to which God is giving spiritual birth, a point Paul expounds in Romans 5 and 6.

Because of Christ's representative role, the narrowing focus of the progress of redemption on to Christ is immediately followed by an explosion outwards. After the ascension of the one individual who died at Calvary and rose again, the Spirit can be poured out on all Christ's followers. Indeed the book of Acts is structured around the Spirit being received by a growing diversity of people, as the ripples expand out from Jerusalem. Hand in hand with this outpouring of the Spirit is the increasingly widespread passing on of the good news about Jesus Christ in verbal form. The Son of God lived one human life in one place at one time. The pattern of his ongoing ministry, now offered to all through his followers, revolves around the Spirit and words.

Jesus implicitly taught his disciples about this in the last week of his life. He prayed to his Father, 'I gave them the words you gave me . . . My prayer is not for them alone. I pray also for those who will believe in me through their message' (John 17:8, 20). This expands the history of divine words becoming human words, outlined in the previous section. For the words God the Father gave to God the Son have been given by the Son, in ordinary human language, to his disciples. Now those words are to be passed on through the words of the disciples. Therefore everyone who never met the Word incarnate directly, but who hears the words of Christ from the disciples, nevertheless encounters the words of the Father and of Christ, who in those words present themselves to us as a covenant-making God.

This theme is also found in Matthew's Gospel. As Jesus sends out the Twelve, according to Matthew, he tells them:

> If anyone will not welcome you or listen to your words, shake the dust off your feet when you leave that home or town. Truly I tell you, it will be more bearable for Sodom and Gomorrah on the day of judgment than for that town. . . . Anyone who welcomes you welcomes me, and anyone who welcomes me welcomes the one who sent me.
> (Matt. 10:14–15, 40)

Thus to reject the disciples' words, which come from Christ and are about Christ, is to reject God, and so to be liable for condemnation. It is easy to be familiar with these words and not to be struck by what lies just below their surface. God has identified himself both with Jesus Christ in person *and* with the passing on by his disciples of the words Jesus brought from the Father, with the result that to reject those human words spoken by the disciples is to reject God. It is only by rejecting God himself that people open themselves up to his condemnation, which is precisely what they did when they rejected human words the disciples brought from Christ.

The same point is made in the parable of the sheep and goats (Matt. 25:31–46). Here the Son of Man saves or condemns people on the basis of kind deeds they have done for 'the least of these brothers and sisters of mine'. One of the key questions of interpretation in this parable is whether this phrase refers to suffering humanity in general, or to Christian disciples in particular, especially those disciples who come bringing the gospel of Christ in culturally hostile circumstances. A study of that phrase and similar phrases throughout Matthew's Gospel suggests very strongly the latter restricted sense.[11] In this parable too, therefore, the rejection of those who come speaking Christ's words is itself a rejection of Christ.

As a final point from the New Testament here, it should be observed that the canonical writings of the apostles anticipate the future beyond their own lifetimes, and prescribe the basis on which the post-apostolic church should continue. Paul describes the covenant community as God's household, 'built on the foundation of the apostles and prophets, with Christ Jesus himself as the chief cornerstone' (Eph. 2:20). The vital bequest of the apostles to subsequent generations of Christians was of course their writings, so Paul in effect draws the closest possible link between the church being founded on Christ *and* founded on the words Christ spoke through the apostles, as set down in their writings. It cannot be the former without also being the latter.

Thus the coming of the Word incarnate does not alter the fact that, for all who come after Christ, human language is the essential medium by which God acts in relation to us and presents himself to us in the offer of a covenant relationship with him in Christ. The final step in this biblical outline will be to draw the link between the words of the Bible and the human language through which God speaks.

God's words and the Bible

So far we have had in view not the Bible in particular but the general proclamation of the words of Christ and of the covenant. Now, though, we need to ask, 'Why equate God's words, and all that that

---

11. See e.g. Donald A. Hagner, *Matthew 14–28*, Word Biblical Commentary 33B (Dallas: Word, 1995), pp. 744–745.

concept entails theologically, supremely with the human words of
the Bible?' For of course it is the case that many theologians who are
happy to speak of the proclamation of the gospel as God's speech
refuse to identify *the Bible in its entirety* as itself the Word of God.

However, it remains impossible to avoid the fact that our only
access to Christ and his words is through the content of the Bible.
When some parts of the Bible are accepted as God's Word, but
others are rejected, the process that usually follows is one where
theologians attempt to draw out of the Bible those sections or
themes that for them express the true Gospel *over against* other
parts of the Bible. This is usually known as discerning 'a canon
within the canon'.[12] Indeed, however radically liberal someone
becomes in their view of Scripture, they usually regard at least
some short phrases from Scripture, such as 'God is love', as accurate expressions in human language of God's real nature.

For the sake of clarity, it is important to point out that this
'canon within the canon' approach is a quite different thing from
the normal recognition that some parts of the Bible do not tell the
whole truth of a matter, for example because they only fore-
shadow a reality that has not yet come. It is also quite different
from acknowledging that certain sections of Scripture are not to
be applied to modern believers exactly as they stand, because a
later stage in the progression of divine revelation has explicitly
superseded them. An example of this is the Old Testament food
laws, which are given a radical reinterpretation by Christ in Mark
7:18–19. By contrast, the 'canon within the canon' approach
involves identifying certain teachings that the Bible really does
affirm, even when appropriately and canonically interpreted, as of
only human origin, and not at all as a word from God. Once this
'canon within the canon', a supposed central core of 'the Word of
God' within Scripture itself, has been identified, it can then be
used as the basis of an 'inner-canonical criticism' of other parts of

---

12. John Goldingay gives a lucid analysis of the different senses that have
    been given to the phrase 'canon within the canon' (John Goldingay,
    Theological Diversity and the Authority of the Old Testament [Grand Rapids:
    Eerdmans, 1987], pp. 122–127).

Scripture, effectively distinguishing between those biblical words through which God does choose to speak and those through which he supposedly does not, because they are thought to be in no way expressive of the gospel.

This strategy is employed especially clearly by the contemporary theologian Wolfhart Pannenberg. He says that the Bible is God's Word only to the extent that it gives expression to the apostolic gospel. He thinks that certain parts of the Bible do that, while others do not. He writes:

> the authority of scripture rests on that of the gospel and its content – the saving presence of God in the person and history of Jesus Christ. Only insofar as they bear witness to this content do the words and sayings of scripture have authority in the church. . . . How far this is true must be tested for each writing and each saying in each writing.[13]

He judges that the New Testament writings can be regarded as inspired Scripture 'only insofar as those writings witness to the Pauline gospel of God's saving activity in Jesus' death on the cross and in his resurrection'.[14] Any part of Scripture that, in his view, falls short of this ought not to be regarded as the authoritative word of God in the church.

The difficulty with this approach is that, since our only access to the gospel of Christ is through Scripture, it is hard to see how a principle of inner-canonical criticism can be discerned that is not arbitrary, being instead determined largely by our own tastes and prejudices. In other words the outcome of any process of 'inner-canonical criticism' is usually a pared-down Bible whose content accords suspiciously well with the insights, obsessions and neuroses of our own culture, and is limited by our own (inevitably inadequate) spiritual experience of our existence in Christ. The suspicion then remains that what is being offered as the 'true' word of God from

---

13. Wolfhart Pannenberg, *Systematic Theology*, vol. 1, tr. Geoffrey W. Bromiley (Grand Rapids: Eerdmans, 1991), p. 463.
14. Wolfhart Pannenberg, 'On the Inspiration of Scripture', *Theology Today* 54 (1997), p. 213.

within the Bible is a human construction, and not divine speech itself. The New Testament scholar Bruce Metzger asserts that

> New Testament scholars have the responsibility as servants of the Church to investigate, understand, and elucidate, for the development of the Christian life of believers, the full meaning of every book written within the canon and not only of those which may be most popular in certain circles and at certain times. Only in such a way will the Church be able to hear the Word of God in all its breadth and depth.[15]

Our only access to the words the Father gave the prophets and his Son, and to the words Christ gave his first disciples, is through the Bible as a whole.

Indeed we find that Christ, towards the end of his earthly life, anticipated a time when his own words would continue to be passed on through the apostolic community. In a highly significant passage, he says to the Twelve:

> I have much more to say to you, more than you can now bear. But when he, the Spirit of truth, comes, he will guide you into all the truth. He will not speak on his own; he will speak only what he hears, and he will tell you what is yet to come. He will glorify me because it is from me that he will receive what he will make known to you. All that belongs to the Father is mine. That is why I said the Spirit will receive from me what he will make known to you. (John 16:12–15)

The key question these verses raise, of course, is this: In what sense did God intend this statement ultimately to be addressed to a wider audience than the original Twelve? If it is addressed *as it stands* ultimately beyond the Twelve, to *every individual believer*, then the resulting situation seems to be the unfortunate one in which all Christians could reasonably claim, of a wide variety of questionable positions they hold, that Christ by the Spirit has led them into that 'truth'. If, though, this teaching is addressed as it stands beyond the

---

15. Bruce M. Metzger, *The Canon of the New Testament: Its Origin, Development, and Significance* (Oxford: Clarendon, 1987), p. 282.

Twelve to *the future church as an institution*, then we are in the equally troublesome situation where the teaching authorities of the church could both add further 'authoritative' revelation to Scripture and interpret Scripture as they wish with impunity. Alternatively, and much more likely, Christ intended these verses to apply, in their fullness, *only to the twelve disciples* (and, by a small extension, as it turns out, to their immediate associates). In other words in this teaching Jesus is anticipating the future communication, through the faithful and obedient work of the Holy Spirit, of words that come from him and that have their ultimate origin in the Father, to the original apostolic community. This lays down part of the theological background to the subsequent writing of the texts that came to form the New Testament by virtue of being recognized as Scripture. It is also the earthly Christ's contribution to our understanding of what is usually called the 'inspiration' of Scripture, which we shall examine in the next chapter. And one further point can be made: this teaching from Christ provides warrant from within the Gospels for the early church's practice of making 'apostolicity' (whether in authorship or source) a vital external criterion in the recognition of certain writings as Scripture and others as not.

In the differing interpretations of John 16:12–15 given above can be recognized a repetition of one of the key issues the main Protestant Reformers faced in the sixteenth century. Does the ongoing authoritative speaking activity of the Holy Spirit reside in the institution of the church as it interprets the Bible, as Roman Catholicism came to say it did? Does it reside in the individual believer, as the Anabaptists of the Radical Reformation of the sixteenth century came to say it did?[16] Or, as the Reformers were

---

16. 'Anabaptist' means 'rebaptizer'. These groups rejected the validity of infant baptism, and insisted on the baptism of adult believers. They had other crucial beliefs about Scripture and the work of the Holy Spirit that marked them clearly off from the mainstream Reformers, which we shall focus on later. Important leaders of the diverse Anabaptist groups included Thomas Müntzer, Conrad Grebel, Jacob Hutter and Menno Simons. The latter two have followers down to the present day who still bear their founder's name: Hutterites and Mennonites.

convinced, does the ongoing authoritative speaking activity of the Holy Spirit take place in and through Scripture, as Scripture is read and as the church thereby finds itself addressed by God through his written Word in the power of the Spirit? This latter answer is the one suggested by the application of John 16:12–15 primarily to the apostolic community alone.

One additional piece of scriptural evidence that these words of Jesus were to be restricted in this way to the apostles is the fact that the later New Testament writings, especially, consciously signal the approaching closure of canonical writing. Thus the Pastoral Epistles, which explicitly face up to the impending post-apostolic period, are characterized *not* by injunctions to future leaders to remain open to whatever words Christ will continue to send from the Father through the Spirit. Instead their focus is on instructing the generation of leaders coming after the apostles to preserve and faithfully pass on the apostolic gospel already delivered (e.g. 2 Tim. 2:2; 3:14). Similarly the book of Revelation ends by closing off the prospect of being extended by further verbal revelation with scriptural status (Rev. 22:18).

The biblical outline offered in this chapter can be summarized fairly simply. God chooses to present himself to us, and to act upon us, in and through human words that have their origin in him, and that he identifies as his own. When we encounter those words, God is acting in relation to us, supremely in his making a covenant promise to us. God identifies himself with his act of promising in such a way that for us to encounter God's promise is itself to encounter God. The supreme form in which God comes to encounter us in his covenant promise is through the words of the Bible as a whole. Therefore *to encounter the words of Scripture is to encounter God in action.* This biblical outline will form the foundation on which subsequent chapters will build, and will determine the shape of our doctrine of Scripture.

3. THE TRINITY AND SCRIPTURE: A THEOLOGICAL OUTLINE

9-14

In this chapter we move to systematic analysis of Scripture as it exists in relation to God, describing Scripture's relationship to each divine person of the Trinity in turn. In some forms of Christian theology the Bible is related in systematic thinking most directly to something other than God himself. For example, in Roman Catholic theology, and also increasingly in some branches of contemporary Protestant theology, Scripture is related primarily to the doctrine of the church. In addition, as noted in the introduction, some evangelical theology, particularly in more popular forms, has offered a systematic doctrine of Scripture as a preliminary discussion about the sources and authorities of Christian truth, prior to explicit treatment of God's nature and actions. This has led to the allegation, not always unfounded, that the resulting doctrine of Scripture appeared to be more an exercise in philosophy than in genuine Christian, that is, Christ-focused and God-oriented, theology. Our first level of systematization therefore relates the Bible to the triune God, rather than to something else, because of the fundamental links between God's person and actions, and his word, which the foregoing chapter outlined.[1]

Of course describing the Bible's relation to each person of the Trinity separately in this way runs the risk of abstraction, as does any kind of trinitarian analysis. Scripture speaks constantly of the unity of God in his actions, and, as theologians have regularly expressed it, all three persons of the Trinity are involved in the actions God performs beyond himself. Nevertheless, as has also often been noted, Scripture itself emphasizes the priority of certain persons within the Trinity in certain divine actions. Thus in the Bible the Father seems to take priority in the act of creation, the Son is the willing and active subject of the incarnation, and the Spirit is the agent of the inspiration of Scripture. Each section of this chapter will take note of those aspects of Scripture most closely related to each person in the Godhead.

Many critics of evangelical and Reformed doctrines of Scripture have been concerned that these doctrines have rushed too quickly from the unsystematic form in which the Bible's relationship to God is described in Scripture to dogmatic statements, thereby producing overly neat systematic forms, most typically under such headings as Scripture's perfection, necessity, sufficiency, clarity, inspiration and authority. Analysis of the Bible under these headings, as the *primary* way in which Scripture is described theologically, does indeed sometimes pass too quickly over the complexity of scriptural testimony and teaching on the nature and function of the Bible in relation to God and his purposes. Or, more subtly, perhaps what has happened is that, although the apparently neat packages of clarity, sufficiency and so on may once have been articulated as the conclusion of a rigorous biblical-theological presentation, a shift then occurred, in which what were previously offered as doctrinal *conclusions* were now

---

1. I am therefore heeding John Webster's helpful warning that some forms of post-Reformation dogmatics unwittingly prepared the way for 'nontheological construals of the Bible' by developing a theological epistemology that was not sufficiently trinitarian (John Webster, 'Hermeneutics in Modern Theology: Some Doctrinal Reflections', *Scottish Journal of Theology* 51 [1998], pp. 323–324).

presented as the *starting point* of what is to be said about the Bible. Consequently the evangelical doctrine of Scripture seemed to many to have become lifeless, devoid of the explicit deep biblical and theological roots that need to remain in place in order to give it spiritual vitality. In fact it is arguable that many who have come to reject the evangelical doctrine of Scripture have done so not so much because they have just found it to be wrong biblically or intellectually incredible, but because they have found the expositions of it which they know of to be lacking in what we might call dynamic spirituality. In the writing of theology there is indeed a need for careful precision; there should also be times when the doctrine is related directly to Christian life and hope lived out in relationship with God.[2]

This chapter offers an outline of a systematization of the biblical material from the previous chapter that attempts to take account of these valid concerns. Thus it is only in the next chapter that terms such as 'the sufficiency of Scripture' and 'the clarity of Scripture' will appear. Here we are still very much engaged in the vital task of describing Scripture explicitly at every point in the light of the character and actions of God, as revealed and witnessed to in Scripture. If readers suspect that concepts such as 'authority', 'sufficiency', 'clarity' and 'necessity' begin to surface in this chapter without being directly named as such, that is because I want to stick with explicitly biblical shapes, concepts and terms for a while yet, not jumping too quickly to doctrinal labels, however tried, tested and truthful they may turn out to be.

The Father and Scripture: the covenant book

In the overarching narrative of Scripture the two great actions of the Father, following the glory of his creative act and the tragedy

---

2. For myself, I find that Bavinck's exposition of the doctrine of revelation contains one of the most spiritually vital doctrines of Scripture I know of, while still being thought through with sharpness and care (Herman Bavinck, *Reformed Dogmatics*, vol. 1, *Prolegomena*, gen. ed. John Bolt, tr. John Vriend [Grand Rapids: Baker Academic, 2003], pp. 283–494).

of the fall of humankind, are to *redeem* and to *reveal*.[3] His repeated acts of redemption lead up to the climactic redemption achieved in Christ's life, death and resurrection. As that history unfolds, God is constantly acting to reveal the meaning of his redemptive acts, and to show people the basis on which they may join the community of those being redeemed. Thus the exodus, as we saw in the previous chapter, would be incomprehensible without words from God explaining its significance. And Scripture, as we also saw previously, is not just a means by which God reveals what his actions signify. It is also one of the redemptive acts by which God draws people into union with Christ and into relationship with himself. Therefore we shall now look at Scripture's role in the Father's work of redeeming and revealing.

Redemption and Scripture

'I will be your God, and you will be my people.' This is the most straightforward form in which God expresses the redemptive relationship he establishes with his people. It is a covenant relationship: a relationship established by means of a promise. Throughout the Bible 'covenant' is the most wide-ranging single description of the way God relates to humankind in his desire to redeem them. The covenant is unilateral and unconditional in its establishment. Of course it is true that in Scripture the means a holy creator provides by which sinful humanity can be reconciled into a covenant relationship with himself are *atonement* and *union with Christ*. Yet these divine acts of atoning for human sin in Christ and of uniting believers with his Son flow out of the fundamentally covenantal nature of the relationship God chooses to establish with us. We are in Christ, redeemed by the cross, because God has acted to bring this about in fulfilment of covenant promises made and recorded in Scripture. God redeems us because in the covenant he has promised to be our God, and to make us his people. Through its various unfolding manifestations in redemption-history, therefore, God's covenant is a single mode

---

3. Indeed, as Bavinck regularly asserts, God's redemptive acts in history *are* his revelation of himself.

of relationship, and the full significance and reality of it unfolds through time.

The death of Christ thus makes sense only as a climax of God's faithfulness to his covenant. Through the prophet Jeremiah God promised he would

> make a new covenant
> with the house of Israel
>   and with the house of Judah . . .
> I will put my law in their minds
>   and write it on their hearts.
> I will be their God,
>   and they will be my people.
> (Jer. 31:31, 33)

The New Testament quotes this passage at length, relating it specifically to what Christ achieved on the cross as simultaneously the great high priest and the once-for-all sacrifice (Heb. 7:23 – 8:13). The same point is evident in the New Testament's narrative accounts of redemption. When one of the criminals crucified alongside Christ confesses both his own crime and Christ's innocence, and implicitly appeals to his messiahship, Christ promises him, 'today you will be with me in paradise' (Luke 23:43). That is a promise made and expressed in covenantal terms drawn explicitly from the Old Testament. The criminal now belongs to Christ, with wickedness and sin forgotten by God (cf. Jer. 31:34).

The covenant which Christ brought to fulfilment was transmitted in written form. It is well known that the covenant at Sinai, as expressed in the Old Testament, bears significant similarities to ancient Near Eastern covenant treaties from the same period, drawn up between an overlord and his subject people; this has been the subject of detailed research.[4] Indeed within the Old

---

4. The work of G. E. Mendenhall and M. G. Kline is usually quoted in this regard. For a brief account see William Sanford La Sor, David Allan Hubbard and Frederic William Bush, *Old Testament Survey: The Message, Form and Background of the Old Testament* (Grand Rapids: Paternoster, 1982), pp. 144–146.

Testament the title 'book of the covenant' was ascribed to both smaller and larger sections of Torah material (Exod. 24:7; 2 Chr. 34:30).[5]

The messianic, redemptive events the New Testament relates fulfil that covenant which God had been establishing from the beginning. As Jesus says before his death, 'We are going up to Jerusalem, and everything that is written by the prophets about the Son of Man will be fulfilled' (Luke 18:31). Christ comes both to uphold and fulfil the Sinaitic law, and its exposition and application in the prophets: 'Do not think that I have come to abolish the Law or the Prophets; I have not come to abolish them but to fulfil them' (Matt. 5:17). His life, in both word and deed, fulfils the covenant. He also, as we saw in the previous chapter, foresees and authorizes the giving of further words from him, beyond his ascension, to the apostolic community through the agency of the Holy Spirit. This is what the early church discerned in those texts it came to regard as scriptural: they bore the necessary marks of being words from the risen Christ, both in their content and because of their authorship from within the early apostolic community. Thus these Christ-given writings, authored by the apostles and their close associates, expounding and applying the meaning of Christ as the fulfilment of the covenant, constitute the New Testament as a whole.

In this light the New Testament constitutes the final chapters of the book of the divine covenant. The Scriptures as a whole constitute the ongoing form in which God makes his covenant promise to his people. They are the means by which the Father articulates the covenant promise he has brought to fulfilment in Christ, which is now to be offered to the whole world, and in which he demonstrates his faithfulness to the covenant through extraordinary ups and downs. The Bible is rightly thought of as fundamentally the book of the inaugurated and fulfilled covenant.

Of course large parts of Scripture are not directly in the form of the declaration of a covenant promise. Therefore, some will ask, is it not rather simplistic to describe the whole collection of

---

5. Peter Jensen develops this point in his *The Revelation of God* (Leicester: IVP, 2002), p. 82.

sixty-six diverse books as one great unified covenant book? What kind of covenant promises from God are expressed in the narratives of Chronicles, or the wisdom sayings of Proverbs? How can psalms addressed *to* God be thought of as words of promise *from* him? However, every literary genre and form within Scripture is linked directly to Scripture's basic covenantal form and function.

Commandments declare the stipulations of the covenant. *Prophecy* and *epistles*, in particular, expound and apply those stipulations in specific contexts; they are, in effect, the covenant preached in different situations. *Narrative* relates the unfolding events in which God's people have successively trusted and rejected him, and through which God has faithfully enacted the consequences of his promises, whether in blessing or judgment. Indeed narrative takes up more space in the Bible than any other literary genre. We might guess that this is because narrative is the form of writing best suited to answering with clarity and conviction the key questions which the offer of a promise always raises: Can I trust the person making this promise? What happens when it seems as if he is failing to keep his promise? What will be the consequences if I trust him, or if I don't? It is answers to these fundamental questions about the covenant that biblical narrative serves to give (see 1 Cor. 10:1–13; Heb. 4:1–13).[6] *Psalms* give exemplary forms in which a believer can address God in many situations in life while remaining faithfully within the covenant, whether one is full of praise for experience of blessing, or confused and despairing over God's apparent failure to keep his promises. And *apocalyptic* writing demonstrates graphically the full reality of the present and ultimate consequences of either blessing or cursing that follow from obedience or disobedience to the covenant.

---

6. Evangelical preachers and theologians are sometimes said to be less comfortable handling biblical narrative than they are with the more didactic and explicitly theological material of the New Testament epistles. However if the reality of God's covenant is central to our lives and thinking, then narrative should strike us as a rather natural form of scriptural writing.

To describe Scripture as 'the book of the covenant' must therefore not be thought of as forcing a complex and rich Scripture
into a one-dimensional theological mould. We must always be suspicious of our tendency to find a convenient way of avoiding the
need to deal with the diversity and complexity of the word God
has given us, turning it into something more manageable that we
can easily comprehend. Yet to see the Bible as 'the book of the
covenant' is not simplistic or reductionist. It is rather to recognize
Scripture's profound role in the relationship between humanity
and God that God wants to establish.

A very high claim for Scripture is of course being made here:
Scripture is an aspect of the action of the sovereign, faithful, self-
revealing God in the world, and specifically it is the action by which
this God declares his ongoing covenant with his people, climaxed in
Christ. Some brands of Christian theology feel that this kind of
claim runs dangerously close to 'divinizing' Scripture (this is the
word that seems to be used most often). The heart of the concern is
that Scripture is being turned into a manifestation of God himself
in the world in such a way that God and his actions are identified
with, and reduced to, human language, syntax and semantics. This, it
is thought, ultimately turns God into another item in the dictionary,
subject to human investigation, just as we might feel that we come
to 'master' Shakespeare by studying his plays and poems. Of course
any human attempt to master God, rather than to be a servant mas-
tered by him, is inexcusable idolatry. There will be more to say about
this criticism of the doctrine I am defending a little further on in
this chapter, but for now it can simply be pointed out that the
description of Scripture as 'covenant book' seems to have been
forced on us by what God says in Scripture both about himself and
about Scripture. True statements about God and his ways can, after
all, often come quite close to error while still expressing important
truth, when they have not yet been fully expounded and refined;
they are not necessarily any less true for that. The history of the
doctrines of the person of Christ and of the Trinity, to mention just
two, makes this clear. It is to be expected that we shall find the same
to be the case with the doctrine of Scripture.

In recent years a few writers on Scripture have appealed to a
branch of the philosophy of language to help us think our way

through this. 'Speech-act theory', as this field of thought is called, proposes a persuasive way of conceiving of what language is and what it is for.[7] It begins by rejecting the widespread notion that language is primarily a logical system for the conveying of bits of information, rather in the way one computer sends data to another. This model of language is commonly assumed to be the correct one whenever human beings are conceived of primarily in terms of their minds and their rationality, as they have often been in Western philosophy since the Enlightenment. By contrast, speech-act theory thinks of language as at root a means by which one person performs actions in relation to another. Every philosophy of language presupposes a certain view of what a human being fundamentally is. The anthropology which speech-act theory most naturally implies is that we are persons, with both

---

7. Seminal speech-act theory texts that have been influential in theology are J. L. Austin, *How to Do Things with Words*, 2nd ed. (Oxford: Clarendon, 1975); John R. Searle, *Speech Acts: An Essay in the Philosophy of Language* (Cambridge: Cambridge University Press, 1969); *Expression and Meaning: Studies in the Theory of Speech Acts* (Cambridge: Cambridge University Press, 1979). Theologians and biblical scholars who have drawn on these works include Anthony Thiselton, Kevin Vanhoozer and Francis Watson. What follows here is drawn particularly from the philosopher and theologian Nicholas Wolterstorff's creative work in his *Divine Discourse: Philosophical Reflections on the Claim that God Speaks* (Cambridge: Cambridge University Press, 1995). Speech-act theory is of course a diverse field. For an analysis of its development from Austin to Searle to Wolterstorff, from a theological perspective, see Timothy Ward, *Word and Supplement: Speech Acts, Biblical Texts, and the Sufficiency of Scripture* (Oxford: Oxford University Press, 2002), pp. 75–105. I should clarify for readers with some knowledge of speech-act theory that I find the ethically focused exposition of speech-act theory given by Nicholas Wolterstorff, which considers speech as it is in the real world, far more truthful and fruitful for theological purposes than the rather different analytical-philosophical approach of the philosopher John Searle. Therefore whenever I speak in this book of 'speech-act theory' I have in mind the Wolterstorff rather than the Searle variety.

body and mind, who perform actions in relation to one another
and to the world around us, which go far beyond the conveying
of information.

The classic example speech-act theorists regularly use to
explain their point is the uttering of a promise. If I say to you the
words 'I promise I'll meet you in town tomorrow,' I have not just
conveyed information; I have enacted something with regard to
the relationship between us. I have put you in the position of
being obliged to trust me. (Of course you may not be obliged to
trust me if you have good reason to think that I am a habitual liar,
or that I shall be unable for some reason to keep my promise.
These 'disqualifiers' do not nullify the basic claim about language
and speech being made here.) And I have acquired for myself the
position of being obliged to you to act in a way that will fulfil my
promise.[8]

This may be a terribly obvious point to make about promises,
but it is also true even of uses of language that, unlike promises,
look like simply the conveying of information. For example, you
might ask me to tell you the time, and I look at my watch and tell
you. That event appears to be no more than the relaying of a piece
of information from one mind to another, but in fact it is far more
than that. If I see you go straight off and ask someone else the
time, I would reasonably conclude, 'Didn't you believe me, then?'
That natural conclusion reveals that language exchange between
people, while of course including the communication of propositions, is fundamentally to do with something different and much
more profound. It is to do with active relationships of trust and
obligation between us.[9] It is not only the dramatic words of, for
example, my wedding vows that oblige me to live within a specific
relationship, to behave in certain ways, and to refrain from certain

---

8. 'Speaking introduces the potential for a whole new range of moral
   culpabilities – and accomplishments. At bottom, it is our dignity as
   persons that requires that we be taken at our word, and take ourselves
   at our word' (Wolterstorff, *Divine Discourse*, p. 94).

9. 'Asserting that so-and-so introduces into human relationships the (prima
   facie) right to be taken at one's word that so-and-so' (ibid., pp. 84–85).

actions. The same is true, perhaps less obviously at first, but just as significantly, of every word we utter.[10]

The strong bonds between ourselves, our actions and the words by which we perform many of our actions is evident in the normal course of life. This is particularly so when we think about the responses that can be made to a promise. For you to say 'I trust you to keep your promise' or 'I trust your promise' or 'I trust your words' is in effect to say the same thing in regard to me. For you to distrust the *words* of my promise is simply to distrust *me*. Persons and actions are so intimately identified in interpersonal relationships that actions begin to look like an extension of our personhood in our relationships with others. This is desperately difficult to map out philosophically (and thankfully that is not our focus here!), but it seems commonsensical to anyone who lives in the real world and thinks a little about how language in fact operates every day of our lives. Much more significantly, of course, it also accords remarkably well with what we saw in the previous chapter of the close relationship in Scripture between God himself, his actions and his words. Of course it is not the case that readers of the Bible failed to notice this until speech-act theorists kindly pointed it out to grateful theologians. It is, rather, that the concepts we are borrowing from speech-act theory can help us discern all the more clearly an aspect of Scripture that has not always been well expounded in the descriptions of the nature and content of Scripture offered by many strands of Christian thought, including evangelical ones.

In this light it is clear that to identify the *words* of a person performing actions with the very *actions* of that person is in fact to do full justice to the nature of language and action as God has made it to be. Conversely, therefore, to distance that person's actions very

---

10. This crucial point makes clear what is often misunderstood about speech-act theory. It offers an overarching description of *all* instances of language use, not just ones that most obviously perform actions (such as wedding vows). And since its account of language relates fundamentally to persons and relationships, a 'speech act' view of language will have profound implications for anthropology and personhood.

far from their words is to do violence to language itself. Even
more seriously, it devalues that person's status as an acting, relating
being who (in the normal course of things) deserves to be taken at
his or her word. To separate me too far from my words is to
mount an attack on me as a person, by pretending that I lack both
the responsibility to be true to my word and the right to be taken
at my word. That is true of speaking persons made in God's
image. It is no less true for God, as we saw in the previous chapter,
in whose image as a speaking God we are made, when he chooses
to act redemptively by means of God-given human language in his
world. In fact there is likely to be an even more profound link
between actions and words in the case of God, because of what
he reveals to be his deep trustworthiness to his word, which far
exceeds any human trustworthiness. The worry that a text written
in human language may wrongly be 'divinized' and idolized may
remain. However, the opposite danger (that of untying God's
actions in the world from the language and meaning of Scripture,
with the inevitable result that his redemptive acts cannot reliably
be known as trustworthy) ought to be much more troubling, since
it is destructive to Christian theology and life.

Revelation and Scripture

The biblical outline offered in the previous chapter led to the conclusion that there are very intimate relationships between God's
words, actions and God himself. I referred to the Old Testament
account of how those who touched the ark of the covenant inappropriately were subject to God's anger, because in some sense the
words carved on the stone tablets were a mode of God's presence
among his people. And those who rejected the apostolic proclamation of the gospel of Christ thereby made themselves liable to
God's condemnation, because in rejecting those words they had
rejected God. Similarly, to hear the words of Christ was directly to
hear the speech of God. It follows that to speak of Scripture as the
book of the covenant, the ongoing form in which God repeats his
covenant promise in the world, ought to lead us to speak of
Scripture as in some sense a mode of God's presence in the world.
In other words the widespread contemporary notion that Scripture
is not itself revelation, but ought instead to be thought of as no

more than a *witness* to revelation, is found to be an inadequate reflection of Scripture's description of its relation to God, to his acts in history and to his people. It is inadequate, whether or not Scripture is taken to be only partially or even wholly reliable as such a witness. This view of the Bible as witness can seem to be standard in modern thought, and is sometimes asserted as if it has already been demonstrated beyond reasonable doubt. Yet it falls short of the relationship between God and his words implied in the covenantal nature of the redemption which God achieves for humanity. The Bible does indeed witness to events and spiritual realities that lie beyond itself, but that is only one aspect of its role in God's hands.

As soon as we find ourselves saying something like this, we ought obviously to realize that we need to tread and think very carefully, in order not to open ourselves up to the kind of idolatry God warns us against so severely in Scripture, and into which humanity falls time and again. For it is idolatrous to identify something that humanity has created with God himself, and thus to give devotion to something that is not the living God. It has sometimes been claimed that the post-Reformation Protestant doctrine of Scripture led precisely to something verging on idolatry. In the last century one of the most eloquent exponents of this criticism was the Swiss theologian Karl Barth. Discussing the doctrine of biblical inspiration as outlined by many seventeenth-century Lutheran and Reformed theologians, Barth judged that 'the statement that the Bible is the Word of God was now transformed . . . from a statement about the free grace of God into a statement about the nature of the Bible as exposed to human inquiry brought under control'.[11] He thought that this evangelical view of Scripture shared deep and surprising roots with the liberal view, which denied the identity of Scripture with the Word of God, and saw Scripture at best as the most profound expression of human religious insight. Both, said Barth, are 'products of the same age and spirit. A common feature is that they both represent means

---

11. Karl Barth, *Church Dogmatics* I/2, tr. G. T. Thompson and Harold Knight (Edinburgh: T. & T. Clark, 1956), p. 522.

whereby Renaissance man tried to control the Bible and also tried
to set up obstacles to stop its controlling him, as indeed it ought to
do.'[12]

Barth's criticisms of the evangelical doctrine of Scripture were
driven in part by his strong desire to protect the uniqueness of the
incarnate Christ as the only instance of the divine uniting per-
manently with the human, the only entity within creation of which
it can truly be said, 'Behold the Lord', without speaking blasphemously. This is an aim with which all orthodox Christian believers
find themselves in deep sympathy. For Barth, as soon as Scripture
has been straightforwardly identified with God's Word, God has
been domesticated, because we can then fool ourselves into thinking that by studying Scripture we can study God. Having identified
God with an object we can master intellectually, we commit the
primordial sin of attempting to exalt ourselves over God. The
truth, though, is that it is always God who grasps hold of us, not
we of him!

Barth's criticisms of the kind of doctrine of Scripture this book
is outlining are serious ones, and are significantly motivated by
orthodox and profound theological concerns. (It is also true
that Barth's doctrine of Scripture was shaped by his acceptance
in principle of many of the conclusions of sceptical scholarship
with regard to the historical value of Scripture, and evangelical
writers are usually critical of this. However, here I want to take
account of his criticisms of the Reformed doctrine of Scripture in
their most orthodox form.) Two sorts of initial response can be
made to Barth, and to those who share his worries about the evangelical doctrine of Scripture. First, as has been outlined, the
equation of Scripture with the Word of God finds clear exegetical
warrant from Scripture itself. This view of Scripture may be
turned all too easily, it is true, by sinful humans into idolatrous
practices by which we deafen ourselves to the voice of God
by assuming that our understanding of Scripture is already complete and needs no reforming by God speaking in Scripture.

---

12. Karl Barth, *Church Dogmatics* I/1, tr. G. W. Bromiley (Edinburgh: T. & T.
    Clark, 1975), pp. 112–113.

What are the implications for preaching, of speech-act theory?

Nevertheless, although it may be abused, it remains a view we are invited into by God himself in Scripture. Evangelicals may at times have expressed and formulated their doctrine of Scripture in a form and with a content that owes too much to post-Enlightenment patterns of thought. However, it is not correct to conclude that they stumbled into their doctrine while following the siren voice of Renaissance humanism away from orthodoxy, hand in hand with liberalism.

For the second response to Barth, I appeal again to speech-act theory. This presents a view of language that, it must again be stressed, is useful theologically only in that it accords well with what arises out of the Bible's own account of God, humanity and language. As we have seen, we as persons who act in relation to one another are so invested in our words that, by speaking, we act upon both ourselves and one another (e.g. in making you a promise I acquire for myself the responsibility to keep my promise and ascribe to you the obligation to take me at my word, other things being equal). It follows that what you do to my words (to my actions as performed by my words) you do to me.

There is, then, a kind of personal presence in the words that someone utters. It is mysterious in some ways, and hard to spell out conceptually, but is nonetheless real. We may call it the 'semantic presence' of persons in their words (in those words as they are used as the means for the performance of actions). We extend the reach of our selves by uttering or writing words that can then travel across a room or around the world, and that, in written or recorded form, can remain beyond our death.[13] This is of course not to say something absurd, such as that to have in your hand a letter from me is the same thing as having me in the room with you. It does, though, take account of the fact that language and

---

13. For the legitimacy of extending the insights of speech-act theory to written language, in contrast to those who make significant distinctions of one kind or another between speech and writing (as do, in different ways, Paul Ricoeur and Jacques Derrida), see Kevin J. Vanhoozer, *Is There a Meaning in This Text? The Bible, the Reader and the Morality of Literary Knowledge* (Leicester: Apollos, 1998); Ward, *Word and Supplement.*

persons, both in their functions and their definitions, are not
nearly so simple when we think hard about them as we might first
suppose they are. Indeed we might suggest that our curious human
ability to extend our selves in relation to one another by means of
our linguistic capabilities has its roots in the fact of our creation in
God's image. For this speaking God, in whose image we are made,
has the unique capacity to be both transcendent and yet present to
us, and this is reflected in a minor way in human linguistic interaction, such that I both am and am not present in the words I say
and write. This is one of the key ways in which our language is an
aspect of God's common grace shown to humanity.[14]

As an aside, it will perhaps be helpful to some readers to relate
these observations about language to issues of language and
meaning in contemporary culture. One of the features of significant areas of Western thought in the last few decades has been the
constant raising of doubt over the ability of language to bear
stable meaning. Most notoriously, thinkers working under the
heading of 'deconstruction' and 'post-structuralism' have sought
to show that any claim that a text 'means' something is just a base-
less attempt by one person to exalt their understanding of it over
what others might want it to mean. In addition, some literary theorists writing under the banner of 'reader-response criticism' have
sought to show that texts do not have meaning in themselves, but
only have whatever meaning readers impute to them. It is now
commonly assumed in many areas of thought in the West that
meaning is not 'out there', but only 'in us'. We do not discover it;
we invent it. It is vital not to miss the underlying fact that this is a
theological issue. If God is not taken into account as the ultimate
solid ground on which all meaning rests, and as the basis on which
our language can be said reliably to bear meaning, then we do

---

14. Thus it is both incorrect and unnecessary to insist, as Barth does, that
    Scripture is not itself the Word of God, but only 'becomes' it. See
    further on this Kevin J. Vanhoozer, 'God's Mighty Speech-Acts: The
    Doctrine of Scripture Today', in Philip E. Satterthwaite and David F.
    Wright (eds.), *A Pathway into the Holy Scripture* (Grand Rapids: Eerdmans,
    1994), pp. 143–181; Ward, *Word and Supplement*, pp. 106–136.

indeed end up staring into the abyss in which meaning is for ever undecidable. It is only a strong commitment to the fact that our linguistic abilities are given to us by God as a reflection of his own character as a speaking God that ultimately provides a satisfactory response to the current crisis of confidence in language and meaning.[15]

Returning to God and Scripture, we might then say that two aspects of God's presence, as Scripture suggests it, are that he is *semantically* present in Scripture, and *personally* present in the person of the Spirit. Thus those, such as Barth, who fear that to identify Scripture with the Word of God is wrongly to identify a human text with God himself have not taken sufficient account of the deep complexities involved in the relationship between persons and language, supremely in the case of God, as he reveals himself in Scripture, and secondarily in the case of his creatures.

To return specifically to Scripture: it is important, in the light of the above, to clarify what is meant here when I speak of *Scripture* as a mode of God's presence. I am not speaking of a physical book. Some traditions of the Christian church, it is true, do venerate a copy of the Bible in their corporate worship, but that has hardly ever, if at all, been a feature of evangelical practice. Nor am I saying that God is present to Christians when the Bible is open and being read, but that he practically disappears when the book is closed, as if somehow the physical opening of a Bible unleashed him like a genie from a bottle. It is probably impossible to find anyone who actually believes this, although evangelicals are sometimes spoken of as if they did, and are sometimes so keen to defend the rightful significance of preaching in the Christian assembly, and of Bible reading for the individual, that they can give the wrong impression that they believe something like this. Neither am I saying that individual words or phrases from the Bible, when read privately or out loud to the gathering of believers, are somehow suffused with divine presence, as if they were the evangelical equivalent of religious relics believed to possess magical powers.

---

15. The best analysis of these issues, with a rich Christian response, is
    Vanhoozer, *Is There a Meaning?*

In order to be clear about what *is* being said, when we say God is semantically present to us in Scripture, we need again to get straight in our minds what kind of a thing our God-given language is. This is crucial, because too many pronouncements by Christians on the Bible, whether in praise of the Bible or out of suspicion of it, are either confused or misleading (or both) on this point. The basic unit of language when it is actually being used in speech and in writing (as opposed to being laid out for analysis in a dictionary) is not the individual word, but the *speech act*.[16] By 'speech act' is meant each act of promising, warning, asserting, congratulating, thanking and so on, as performed by means of language. A speech act can be as short as a single word ('Go!'), or as long as a unified collection of books (the Bible as God's covenant promise in writing). Therefore when we speak of Scripture as a mode of God's presence, we are asserting that it is in the *speech acts* of Scripture that God reveals himself by being semantically present to us, as he promises, warns, rebukes, reassures and so on. And this revelation is happening when the words of Scripture are read: when God is performing again, through the reading of Scripture, the same action he performed through those words when they were first written.[17]

If God has not identified both his person and actions with the speech acts of Scripture, then we do not have a God whom we can

---

16. In fact, of course, even dictionaries do not give fixed meanings for individual words, but are selective archives of words *as they have been used in real life* (as the larger dictionaries make explicit by the use of quotations), and from which the reader must make a choice regarding the word in the particular context in which he wants to understand it.

17. Lest it be thought I am saying God is present in the force or intention of Scripture but not in its propositions, we should stress that any speech act is made up both of 'illocutionary force' (a speech-act term, referring to what is being done through the words), and of propositional content (what is being said in the words). Each of these is an abstraction of the unified reality of a speech act. Thus in the case of Scripture God is semantically present in both. This will become important further on, when I discuss biblical inerrancy.

know and trust in any meaningful sense, because he cannot then be said to have revealed himself through a covenant we can come to understand and trust. Yet the very nature of God as a promise-giver means he chooses to present himself to us in Scripture in a form that of course we can presumptuously and sinfully abuse if we so choose, just as it was tragically possible for God, once he had taken human flesh, to be persecuted by his own creatures. However, just as the humiliated God incarnate was the very means of our redemption, so too without Scripture as I have outlined it God would not be the God of promise he chooses to be for us.[18]

The Son and Scripture: the words of the Word

Jesus and the Bible as both 'Word of God'

It is a striking feature of the New Testament's description of the second person of the Trinity that he is designated as 'the Word': 'In the beginning was the Word [*logos*], and the Word was with God, and the Word was God' (John 1:1). As has been well documented, the Greek term *logos* was widely used in ancient philosophy, and had a range of meanings that extended far wider than simply language-related ones such as 'word' or 'message'. However, the referents of the term at the beginning of John's Gospel must include linguistic ones, since the use of *logos* in the context of the Gospel is more biblical than it is Greek. John is referring much more directly to the meanings of the phrase 'the Word of God' in the Old Testament than he is to the usages of *logos* in Greek thought. If he intends to allude to the latter, he is wanting to subsume those Greek notions into the more truthful and all-encompassing reality of Jesus Christ, and in so doing transform them.

---

18. For a helpful exposition of this point as central to the concerns of the Protestant Reformers, especially Calvin, see Carl Trueman, 'The God of Unconditional Promise', in Paul Helm and Carl Trueman (eds.), *The Trustworthiness of God: Perspectives on the Nature of Scripture* (Leicester: Apollos, 2002), pp. 175–191.

As noted in the biblical outline in the previous chapter, the
'Word of God' in the Old Testament operates at times as a func-
tional equivalent of 'God himself', or of 'God in action in the
world'. This curious feature of the Old Testament has consider-
able light cast on it when God himself, in the person of the Son,
designated as 'Word', takes to himself human flesh and lives,
speaks and acts in the world. He appears as the one who is God in
person, God's Word in human form, and God in action. 'Word' in
the Old Testament comes then to be seen as one of the seeds of
what later grew into the New Testament understanding of the plurality of persons within the one God. The doctrine of the Trinity
could never have been derived exclusively from the Old Testament
itself, and the New Testament provides fresh revelation of the Son
and the Spirit. Yet with hindsight this new revelation makes profound sense of the veiled ways in which the Old Testament speaks
of God's action in terms of 'Word' and 'Wisdom'.

Moreover, 'word' and 'word of God' continue in the New
Testament, after Christ's ascension, as descriptions of the apostolic message of God's saving action in Jesus Christ. A typical text
in this regard is 1 Thessalonians 2:13, where Paul tells the
Thessalonian believers that he thanks God that they received his
message 'not as a human word, but as it actually is, the word of
God'.[19] We may rightly feel some theological nervousness in saying
that Scripture simply is the Word of God, for fear of com-
promising the unique identity of Christ as the Word of God.
Notwithstanding these concerns, this scriptural language about
'word' should make us wary of leaping too quickly into systematized statements that the Bible is *not* itself the Word of God,
however proper our motive. We should let our thinking and our
descriptions of the Bible be shaped rather more by Scripture, and
at least at this point God in the Bible gives some warrant for us to
apply the phrase 'Word of God' as readily to the Bible as we do to
Christ. How we can do so and not at the same time fatally com-
promise the unique devotion owed to Christ with a misplaced

---

19. See also Acts 4:31; 6:2; 8:4, 14 (drawn from J. I. Packer, *'Fundamentalism'
and the Word of God* [London: Inter-Varsity Fellowship, 1958], p. 42).

veneration of a religious book is a vital distinction that needs to be made, and to which I shall come shortly.

I need here, though, to say a little more about how Scripture comes close to referring to God and to the message of Scripture in equivalent terms. A writer who has expounded this point with clarity is the influential American theologian of the late nineteenth and early twentieth centuries, B. B. Warfield. He notes especially two different ways in which Scripture expresses this: 'In one of these classes of passages the Scriptures are spoken of as if they were God; in the other, God is spoken of as if he were the Scriptures.' In the former category is Romans 9:17, which ascribes to 'Scripture' words that in fact, as narrated in the book of Exodus, were spoken by God ('For Scripture says to Pharaoh: "I raised you up for this very purpose, that I might display my power in you"'). It is clear that, for Paul in Romans, to speak of the words of Scripture is not to refer to a lesser authority than to speak of the words of God. Conversely in Matthew 19:4–5 Jesus puts into the mouth of 'the Creator' some words from Genesis that in their original context are in fact not quoted as uttered by God, but form part of the narrative ('"Haven't you read", he replied, "that at the beginning the Creator 'made them male and female,' and said, 'For this reason a man will leave his father and mother and be united to his wife, and the two will become one flesh"'?'). 'The two sets of passages, together', concludes Warfield, 'thus show an absolute identification, in the minds of these writers, of "Scripture" with the speaking God.'[20]

A similar point is evident in some of Christ's words to his disciples shortly before the crucifixion. He urges them, 'Remain in me, as I also remain in you . . . If you remain in me and I in you, you will bear much fruit' (John 15:4–5). Then immediately he says, 'If you remain in me *and my words* remain in you, ask whatever you wish, and it will be done for you. This is to my Father's glory, that you bear much fruit, showing yourselves to be my disciples' (vv. 7–8; italics added). The repetition of 'bear much fruit' from verse 5 shows that

---

20. B. B. Warfield, *The Inspiration and Authority of the Bible* (Philadelphia: Presbyterian & Reformed, 1948), pp. 299–300.

in verse 7 Jesus has not moved from his theme of the mutual 'remaining' of himself and his disciples in each other. The switch in verse 7 to his *words* remaining in them thus appears to be synonymous in Jesus' mind with Jesus himself remaining in them. This is a striking example of the near identity, in the disciples' relationship with Christ, of relating to his words and relating to Christ himself.

Furthermore it is often pointed out that Luke, at the beginning of the book of Acts, the second volume of his canonical work, hints strongly at his conviction that the events he was about to narrate were ultimately actions which Christ was *continuing* to perform, now risen and ascended ('In my former book, Theophilus, I wrote about all that Jesus *began* to do and to teach . . .', Acts 1:1; italics added). In that light the book of 'the Acts of the Apostles' could also be entitled 'the continuing acts of Jesus Christ, through the Holy Spirit'. Analogously, the use of identical terminology ('word') in Scripture for Christ and for the apostolic message about him suggests that we can rightly think of Scripture as the book of 'the continuing words of Jesus Christ, given through the Holy Spirit'. This is strengthened when we remember the provision Jesus made for the communication of further words from him to the disciples after the outpouring of the Spirit, in John 16:12–15 (discussed in the previous chapter). Consequently the words of Jesus Christ, the written New Testament, can be identified with the ongoing semantic activity of the risen Christ in the world.

This is the biblical-theological basis on which we ascribe the phrase 'Word of God' to both Christ and the Bible. It is quite right to say, as J. I. Packer does, that 'God's revelation is called his "Word" because it is reasoned verbal discourse which has God as its subject and its source.'[21] It is also true to argue that we cannot be loyal to Christ as the Word of God while rejecting his view of Scripture as the written Word of God, as expressed in such texts as John 10:34–35, as Donald Macleod points out.[22] Similarly we

---

21. J. I. Packer, *God Has Spoken*, 2nd ed. (London: Hodder & Stoughton, 1993), p. 72.

22. Donald Macleod, *A Faith to Live by: Understanding Christian Doctrine* (Fearn, Ross-shire: Mentor, 1998), p. 14.

should not overlook the simple point made in the seventeenth century by the Genevan theologian Francis Turretin, in his rejection of the Catholic argument, based on Matthew 23:8, that Christ, not Scripture, should be our teacher. Turretin's response was that 'Christ is our only teacher, in such a sense as that the ministry of the word is not thereby excluded, but necessarily included because now in it only he addresses us and by it he instructs us.'[23] However, our most fundamental reason for speaking of both Christ and the Bible as 'Word of God' is that the speech acts related in Scripture are the means by which Christ continues to present himself as a knowable person in the world. The Dutch theologian Herman Bavinck, writing a century ago, puts the point in this typically striking way: '[Scripture] is the product of God's incarnation in Christ and in a sense its continuation, the way by which Christ makes his home in the church, the preparation of the way to the full indwelling of God.'[24] Scripture's words are 'Word' not just because he sent them and speaks through them, but also because its words are his actions, the present word-actions of the Word.

Yet in making this rather extraordinary claim we are not of course saying (as indeed has never been seriously said) that Christ and the Bible are 'Word of God' in precisely the same sense. My words, and the actions I perform by means of them, are in some sense to be identified with me, yet it is clear that my words are not identical with me, but (in a hard-to-define but nevertheless true and real sense) go out from me as an extension of my self in relationship with others. So too Scripture is related to the person of Christ as the means of his acting in the world and of his self-presentation to us in such a fundamental way that it is appropriate to call both him and Scripture 'Word'. Yet in saying this we do not necessarily confuse the person with the book. A book is not a person and a person is not a book; the necessary

23. Francis Turretin, *Institutes of Elenctic Theology*, vol. 1, *First Through Tenth Topics*, tr. George Musgrave Giger, ed. James T. Dennison, Jr. (Phillipsburg: Presbyterian & Reformed, 1992), 2.2.12.
24. Bavinck, *Reformed Dogmatics*, vol. 1, pp. 380–381.

safeguards to ordering 'Christ as Word' and 'Bible as Word'
appropriately in relation to each other are already there in this
rather obvious fact.

It is the person of Christ who is primarily the Word. He is
spoken of directly in those terms in Scripture; he is 'the Word of
life' (1 John 1:1). Christ is the one in whom the person of the Son
was incarnated in an unrepeatable union of two natures, divine
and human. He is the one who was conceived supernaturally, died
a substitutionary death, rose physically and ascended to the right
hand of the Father, and in whom the life of the believer is hidden
(Col. 3:3). It is to him that our devotion is due, and it is he who
will be exalted for eternity as the Lamb who was slain for our
redemption. No Bible is referred to in the Bible's apocalyptic
vision of the new creation, because the dwelling of the Father
and the Son with renewed humanity will be sufficiently intimate,
presumably, to make Scripture unnecessary for life in relationship
with God (Rev. 22:3–5). The transience of Scripture, the fact that
it serves to lead us to be part of the renewed creation, at which
point it will fall away, is a fundamental theme in Bavinck's doctrine of Scripture: 'Like the entire revelation, Scripture, too, is a
passing act.'[25]

Yet Scripture is also rightly referred to directly as the Word of
God, but in a secondary sense, because of its servant-like relation
to Christ. (At one point Bavinck calls Scripture 'the handmaiden
of Christ'.[26] Indeed Scripture as the *servant* of Christ is a constant
theme in his writing.) Scripture is related to the Son in the same
way the covenant promise is related to the person of the Father, as
a means of his action in the world, and thereby also a kind of
extension of himself into the world in relation to us. We should
read, listen to and hear it preached, in order to find ourselves presented again with Christ and addressed by him. As we encounter
the words of Scripture, we are encountering the Son in action, presenting himself to us in his call on us to take up our cross and
follow him. Given that this is so, it would actually be a curious

---

25. Ibid., p. 381.
26. Ibid., p. 440.

thing if the Bible and Christ were held so separate from each other that they were *not* to be designated by the same phrase. If we are unwilling to think of Scripture unambiguously as 'the Word of God', we distance Christ from the Scripture by which he presents himself to us so that we may know him. Consequently the suspicion will be hard to shift that in knowing Christ through Scripture we may not actually be in communion with God as he really is. Scripture testifies to a real, ontological relationship between the Son and his words written in Scripture. Therefore we ought not to shy away from the terminology God himself has given us in Scripture to allow us to come to terms with that profound relationship between Christ as Word and Scripture as Word.

What then can we say about the fear that through this kind of doctrine of Scripture we might come to venerate Scripture as 'the Word of God' in a way that detracts from Christ as Saviour and Lord? First of all, any motivation to defend the uniqueness of Christ's identity is praiseworthy. Yet what is most likely envisaged by those who express this fear is the kind of practice that seems to draw perverse delight from debating minor details of biblical interpretation, while simultaneously ignoring Christ's teaching on, for example, love for one's neighbour. This is similar, as is often pointed out, to the Pharisees' treatment of their Scriptures (our old Testament) and Christ directed some of his harshest condemnation at people like these (Matt. 23, esp. vv. 23–24). This kind of usage of Scripture can of course be encountered in evangelical churches, for example when someone with a vicious tongue in private but impeccable doctrine in public is appointed to a leadership position in church, or when one kind of sin (such as sexual immorality) is roundly condemned, while another kind (say, gossiping, or lack of hospitality) is overlooked.

However, the root of this sorry problem, where it occurs, is not a faulty doctrine of Scripture. It is rather that a right doctrine has been applied only piecemeal to Christian life and thinking. In particular, there is often at root a wrong interpretation from the content of Scripture itself, of what Scripture's aim is. God's aim in Scripture is to lead us to true devotion to Christ, and obedience to him and love for him, impinging on every area of life and thought. Scripture's aim is also, as Bavinck regularly says, to take us from sin to eternal glory.[27] Therefore the right solution is not to propose a doctrine of Scripture that moves away from the testimony God gives in Scripture regarding the nature of Scripture, for that would separate the authority of Christ from those words of his that in fact need to be brought to bear with greater authority. The right way forward is rather to pay more appropriate attention to the content, form and aims of Scripture as God has in fact given it to us. It was just in this way that Christ challenged the Pharisees in their dangerously short-sighted reading of their Scriptures. He did not attempt to downgrade their understanding of the full divinity of their Scriptures, but in fact at every point upheld such a high view of the Scriptures. Instead he urged them to read their Scriptures again, but this time more fully and wisely. He is recorded on a number of occasions asking them, and others of his devout Jewish opponents, 'Haven't you read . . . ?' (Matt. 12:3, 5; 19:4; 21:16, 42; 22:31). Paying full and wise attention to Scripture as the written Word of God is crucial if we wish to worship and follow the Word-made-flesh, the Son of God, rightly.

Scripture and the incarnation

Scripture's speech acts may be God in action by means of language, but they are also the writings of fallen human beings in real situations in the world. Thus a fundamental question rightly raised is: How should we think of the interrelationship of the divine and human characteristics of Scripture? A fuller answer to this question will be given in the subsequent section on Scripture and the Holy Spirit. Yet the question needs to be raised initially in this discussion of Scripture's relationship to Christ, because many writers on Scripture have wondered whether the incarnation of the Son of God is a helpful analogy for understanding the relationship between the divine and human aspects of Scripture. Might the way

---

27. 'The revelation of Scripture makes known to us another world, a world of holiness and glory. This other world descends into this fallen world, not just as a doctrine but also as a divine power . . . [which leads this world] out of the state of sin, through the state of grace, to the state of glory' (ibid., p. 376).

in which the divine and human interrelate in *Christ* help us to understand how the divine and human aspects of *Scripture* interrelate? There is no doubt that the Bible is quite thoroughly human. It was written by people using their powers of historical research (see Luke 1:1–4), as well as their spiritual insight, prophetic courage, literary artistry and personal conviction. In its humanness in this regard Scripture seems to be analogous to the full human nature the Son took on. And evangelical doctrines of Scripture have also always spoken of the Bible as 'fully divine', just as Christ was fully divine. Since the traditional orthodox theological language about Christ is that he is 'one person with two natures', does it therefore help to speak of the Bible, borrowing that description of Christ, as 'one book with two natures, one human and one divine'?

In debates in the mid-twentieth century in the United Kingdom, liberal theologians accused evangelicals, as they have often done, of denying Scripture's true humanity, alleging that this was analogous to the heresy of denying that Jesus Christ had a fully human nature. This was a claim to the effect that evangelicals lost sight of Scripture's fully human characteristics, blurring them with its divine ones. Evangelicals responded that their view of Scripture was in fact analogous with the orthodox doctrine of Christ's person as constituting two natures, without these being either held in separation or intermingled. They in turn laid at the liberals' door the charge of making a mistake with regard to Scripture analogous to the Christological heresy of the Nestorians of the early church, who thought of Christ as comprising not two natures but two *persons*, one human and one divine. In other words the liberals were distinguishing too sharply between the Bible as a human book and as the means of divine communication.[28]

In fact this kind of analogy between Scripture and incarnation is of very limited value. As many writers have acknowledged, the union of divine and human natures in the incarnation is by its very nature unique, and so can be appealed to only tentatively as an analogy, and its usefulness as such will be severely curtailed. In

---

28. See Packer, *'Fundamentalism'*, pp. 82–84.

particular the human and divine *actions* that in some way interact in the production of Scripture are not usefully comparable with the human and divine *natures* that unite in the person of Christ. A 'nature' and an aspect of interpersonal linguistic action are rather different entities.

One contemporary theologian, John Webster, has questioned, as have others before him, the legitimacy of appealing to incarnational analogy to elucidate Scripture, but this time on a different basis. He argues thus:

> the application of an analogy from the hypostatic union can scarcely avoid divinising the Bible by claiming some sort of ontological identity between the biblical texts and the self-communication of God. Over against this, it has to be asserted that no divine nature or properties are to be predicated of Scripture; its substance is that of a creaturely reality (even if it is a creaturely reality annexed to the self-presentation of God); and its relation to God is instrumental.[29]

In the subsequent pages of his book, Webster repeatedly rejects the ascription to Scripture of 'divine properties', which seems to be what he means by 'divinising the Bible'. Although Webster's book is full of subtle and insightful thought, at this crucial point he is not as careful with his concepts as he needs to be. We need to ask: If the Bible is being vaunted (or rejected) as 'a divine text', what precisely is being claimed (or denied)? It is of course not the claim that God has communicated divine attributes to a paper-and-ink form of the Bible. No sensible Christian has ever claimed that.

Therefore when we speak about divine 'properties' or 'nature' of a 'text', what indeed are we talking about? The only useful sense in which this can be meant is something like this: 'the personal origin, purpose and content ['properties' or 'nature' in this sense] of the interpersonal speech acts which the words of that text constitute ['text' in this sense]'. The nature of language, including

---

29. John Webster, *Holy Scripture: A Dogmatic Sketch* (Cambridge: Cambridge University Press, 2003), p. 23.

God's speech, is that of a means of interpersonal communicative action, and not a 'thing' with 'properties'. We are not then faced with choosing, as Webster seems to place us, to regard Scripture's relation to God as either instrumental, or sharing in divine 'properties' or 'nature' that belong properly to God alone. That is in fact to ask us to choose between two options that both borrow more from the idea of the Bible as 'a thing' than they do from the reality of the Bible as the means of God's interpersonal communicative action with us. An 'instrument' for the declaration of a covenant by the covenant-making God of Scripture will inevitably share in some of the 'nature' and 'properties' of that God. That follows from the character of God, from the nature of redemption for us that he has chosen, and from the qualities of the people, language and actions he has chosen to create.

An underlying problem in Webster's discussion may be that, in repeating the word 'text' as applied to Scripture in our analytical descriptions of it (as Webster does, and as many contemporary writers do), we can be led to forget what language in fact is and is for. To call something a 'text' can perhaps make it easy to think of it as an object laid in front of our critical gaze. However, to refer to something as a 'word' or a 'message' more obviously treats it as a means of encounter with the communicative action of another person. Consequently we end up regarding Scripture more as an object than as an instance of language in use, and thus we seek to judge between descriptions of it according to categories of 'properties' it may or may not possess, which are more suitable to descriptions of objects in the world than they are to a means of personal interaction.[30]

To say that Jesus Christ is divine is to say, in traditional orthodox categories, that in him a fully divine nature was united with a fully human nature, without separating or confusing the two. To say

---

30. This is ironic, since one of the key points of Webster's book is rightly to critique those strands of Protestant theology that described Scripture in relative isolation from the doctrines of God and redemption. Indeed in many other ways his book does successfully and profoundly think of Scripture, as he wishes to, as 'holy'.

that the Bible is divine is appropriate and necessary, but is to make an entirely different kind of claim, because in the case of the Bible we are attempting to describe not a person but a set of interpersonal communicative actions. To speak of Scripture as in itself divine is therefore to speak of the divine origin of the *speech acts* of Scripture, a characteristic that follows from their identity as *God's* speech acts. To say that Scripture is divine is not to say *less* than this, because that would drive an unwarranted and destructive wedge between Christ and his words. Yet neither is it to say *more* than this, since to identify Scripture as the Word of God does not exalt it in competition with the union of divine and human natures in the person of Christ.

Our progress in this theological outline thus far might be summarized in this way. To speak of 'Scripture' is to speak of the speech acts performed by means of the words of Scripture. Scripture is the covenant promise of the Father in written form. Because of the unity of the Father and the Son in revelation and redemption, Scripture is at the same time the word by which the incarnate and ascended Word, the one in whom all God's covenant promises are fulfilled, continues to act and to present himself semantically so that he may be known in the world over which he has all authority. This begins to express what we have meant by describing Scripture as an act of the triune God. Therefore we now come to think through the relation of Scripture to the third person of the Trinity, the Holy Spirit.

9-25

The Holy Spirit and Scripture: the God-breathed Word

There are three primary actions of the Holy Spirit with regard to Scripture. First, he is the agent of God's *authoring* of Scripture. It was through him that God gave the words that the writers of the Bible wrote.[31] Secondly, because the Spirit is

---

31. For the sake of simplicity, I shall refer in this section to Bible *writers*. This can be taken to include any subsequent editors of biblical material. The extent to which certain biblical texts might have undergone small-scale editorial processes is not our concern here.

himself the living God, he also *preserves* Scripture providentially from one generation to the next. Thirdly, in the present he is the one who opens minds to *comprehend* and hearts to *trust* what God says in Scripture. These three actions (traditionally termed respectively *inspiration, preservation* and *illumination*) will be explored here.

The inspiration of Scripture

The Spirit as the author of Scripture

A relatively small group of Bible passages is regularly referred to when the question of the inspiration of Scripture arises: primarily 2 Timothy 3:16, particularly alongside 2 Peter 1:20–21. It is important to point out that these passages are not scattered and isolated statements on which an entire doctrine of Scripture is rather precariously built, like an upside-down pyramid balancing on a molehill. This is sometimes alleged against the evangelical doctrine of Scripture, and the biblical outline presented in the previous chapter is partly intended to demonstrate that these commonly cited verses in fact express what Scripture constantly teaches and assumes. That is, the words (or better: the speech acts) of Scripture originate not ultimately from human spiritual insight but from the mind of God.

The Holy Spirit was God's agent in the giving of words to the Old Testament prophets: 'prophecy never had its origin in the human will, but prophets, though human, spoke from God as they were carried along by the Holy Spirit' (2 Pet. 1:21). There is a clear hint here that the divine origin of prophecy did not erase its genuinely human form. Indeed even a cursory reading of Old Testament prophecy shows that, for example, Isaiah, Jeremiah and Ezekiel wrote in ways that naturally expressed their very different characters and temperaments. Yet the main emphasis of these verses is on the passivity of the people who spoke God's words; they were, says Peter, 'carried along'. As we shall see, theologians have regularly stressed that this passivity is to do with the *origin* of the words, the fact that humans did not invent them. It says very little about the *mechanism* by which human and divine wills might have worked together in the composition of these words.

Similarly with the New Testament, in John 16:12–15 Jesus promises that the Spirit is the one who will convey to the apostles further words he has to teach them, beyond his ascension. The stress is again on the passivity of the apostles as the recipients rather than originators of these words. This passage is sometimes passed over too quickly in discussions of biblical inspiration. However, it is a crucial one, because it makes clear that the Spirit's role in authoring Scripture is essentially not that of a creative writer in his own right, but that of an agent of the words of Christ. Although we are speaking about the Spirit as the immediate divine author of Scripture, we could just as easily say that Christ is its author.[32] And in fact in this same passage Christ says that all his words originate from the Father, and therefore authorship can be ascribed to him also. Such is the nature of the trinitarian activity of God in the world.

This role for the Holy Spirit in relation to Scripture is expressed most succinctly in 2 Timothy 3:16, in the phrase 'all Scripture is God-breathed'. The Spirit is not named directly here, but his activity is strongly alluded to in the Greek adjective used by Paul to describe Scripture, *theopneustos*. This word is made up of *theos* (God) and *pneuma* (which can be translated, among other things, 'breath', 'spirit' or 'Spirit'). This verse thus expresses the activity of the Holy Spirit within the action of God in typical biblical fashion, ascribing to him the role of agent and minister of God's purposes.

Theopneustos was traditionally translated in English Bibles by the word 'inspired'. This choice of translation was influenced by the Latin translation of the Bible, the Vulgate, which spoke of Scripture in this verse as *inspirata*. However, for a long time now most commentators have been convinced that 'God-breathed', a translation adopted by the New International Version and other versions, is a much better rendering of *theopneustos* than 'inspired'.

---

32. Calvin captures this point well, saying that the apostles wrote 'from the Lord, that is, with Christ's Spirit as precursor' (John Calvin, *Institutes of the Christian Religion*, Library of Christian Classics, vols. 20–21, ed. John T. McNeill, tr. Ford Lewis Battles [Philadelphia: Westminster, 1960], 4.8.8).

This translation makes clear that this verse speaks not of God's 'inspiring' action in the minds and lives of the authors of the Bible, but instead of <u>his 'expiration', his breathing out, of the words of Scripture</u>. In other words 2 Timothy 3:16 proclaims that the Bible's words are entirely God's words. It is teaching about the divine origin of the Bible, and not about the way in which humans came to cooperate with God in writing those words down.

This was expounded famously and at length a century ago by B. B. Warfield. He summarized the implications of Scripture as *theopneustos* with the phrase <u>'what Scripture says, God says'</u>.[33] Whenever a phrase like this is used, some will imagine that Warfield is representative of those who read Scripture without paying any heed to the literary, canonical and historical context in which a phrase occurs. However, Warfield of course had a sophisticated approach to the interpretation of Scripture, and knew how to interpret it appropriately. When he speaks of 'what Scripture says', he means 'Scripture as properly interpreted'.

Warfield's study of ancient Greek language and literature demonstrated convincingly that *theopneustos* refers to the Bible's origin, and not, as some contemporaries of his claimed, to the 'inspiring' effects it had on its readers, nor to the activity of God in 'inspiring' its authors to write such words.[34] He notes that Reformed theology in general and, most strikingly, the influential Westminster Confession of Faith (1646) assert the *fact* of inspiration, while leaving the *mode* of inspiration as something 'inscrutable'.[35] This is in line with 2 Timothy 3:16, which asserts that 'the Scriptures are a Divine product, without any indication

---

33. It has been alleged that Warfield's doctrine of Scripture was in significant ways an innovation, and not truly representative of the doctrine of the Protestant Reformers; e.g. Jack B. Rogers and Donald K. McKim, *The Authority and Interpretation of the Bible: An Historical Approach* (San Francisco: Harper & Row, 1979). This work provoked a detailed and largely successful rebuttal from John D. Woodbridge, *Biblical Authority: A Critique of the Rogers/McKim Proposal* (Grand Rapids: Zondervan, 1982).
34. Warfield, *Inspiration and Authority*, pp. 245–296.
35. Ibid., p. 420.

of how God has operated in producing them'.[36] It is also the same as Calvin's approach, since the Reformer also focused on Scripture's origin, not the mode of its composition.[37]

Some have argued that there is a clear difference between Calvin and later Reformed theologians on this question. Calvin, it has been said, regards the 'divineness' of Scripture as resting on God's personal acts of revelation to certain people by speaking to them; much of this was passed on orally, only later coming to be written down. Later theologians by contrast, runs the argument, focus their support for the divinity of Scripture entirely on inspiration understood as the actual moment of the composition of the writings of Scripture. (An influential exponent of this view of the history of Reformed theology was the nineteenth-century German writer Heinrich Heppe.[38]) It may be true that post-Reformation writers have more to say in their systematic writings about the act of the writing of Scripture than do their forebears in the Reformation, but that is an aspect of theological exposition, and not innovation. All major Reformed writers on the topic, from Calvin through to Warfield, are agreed that the main thrust of the doctrine of inspiration is that the words of Scripture have their origin in God. Whether the focus of interest in the means by which God acted in the production of Scripture should be on prior events in the writer's life, where God through the Spirit spoke to him words he later wrote, or on the actual moment of composition, is a secondary matter, over which differences of emphasis do not count for a great deal. We may judge with the benefit of hindsight that in the seventeenth and eighteenth centuries too much speculation arose in some quarters over

---

36. Ibid., p. 133.

37. 'Whether God became known to the patriarchs through oracles or visions or by the work and ministry of men, he put into their minds what they should then hand down to their posterity' (Calvin, *Institutes* 1.6.2).

38. Heinrich Heppe, *Reformed Dogmatics: Set Out and Illustrated from the Sources*, rev. and ed. Ernst Bizer, tr. G. T. Thompson (Grand Rapids: Baker, 1950), pp. 14–21.

the mechanics of divine authorship through human authors.[39] However, it remains true that even in the late nineteenth century B. B. Warfield, usually thought of as a direct descendent of post-Reformation theologians, takes good account in his doctrine of inspiration of God's revelatory acts to individuals, preceding the actual writing of those words in Scripture.[40] Bavinck speaks in very similar terms to Warfield about how the Spirit's actions in the Bible writers at the moment of the composition is the natural climax of a long process of the Spirit's preparation of the writers through their 'birth, upbringing, natural gifts, research, memory, reflection, experience of life, revelation, etc.'[41]

It is clear from all this that the action of God referred to by *theopneustos* does not mean anything close to what is meant by the English word 'inspire' in normal usage. This is regularly pointed out in studies of biblical inspiration, but it needs constantly to be repeated because, though not hard to grasp, it is often overlooked in discussions of inspiration. 'Inspire' in normal English usage refers to the impact one person has upon another, enabling them to perform something they might not otherwise have achieved. The theological use of the term, however, speaks only about the origins of the words of the Bible, not the manner of its authoring, and not its effects on readers. Consequently it is arguable that we should drop the term 'the inspiration of Scripture', as the phrase so easily leads to confusion. However, it is now so standard that it is impractical to suggest changing it; it is therefore all the more important to remember the sense of *theopneustos* in 2 Timothy 3:16.

---

39. The most commonly quoted consequence of this tendency is the view some came to hold, but that few would hold today, that the vowel pointing of the Hebrew text of the Old Testament was also God-breathed (see ibid., pp. 19–20).
40. Warfield, *Inspiration and Authority*, pp. 71–102.
41. Bavinck, *Reformed Dogmatics*, vol. 1, p. 438. This is an aspect of what Bavinck calls 'organic' inspiration, his key term for his understanding of inspiration. The differences between him and Warfield at this point lie much more in the area of tone and style than in substance and content.

This kind of confusion can be illustrated by some recent writing on inspiration. A number of writers, who for a variety of reasons have concluded that the Bible does not have its origins entirely in God, expound 'inspiration' as a reference to the way in which God inspiringly guided the Bible writers to write as they did. Cast in these terms, God's actions on the Bible writers does not seem especially unique, since his role is to prompt and nudge, rather than to speak, and so it is often said that we must think of God communicating and 'inspiring' people in similar ways in the present.[42] Others take inspiration as a statement not about the Bible itself, nor of God's action in producing it, but about the church's experience in finding that it is led to salvation through Scripture. Scripture is then said to be 'inspired' in the sense that Christians find it spiritually inspiring.[43] These approaches all have in common the fact that they theologize about 'inspiration' with little reference to careful linguistic study of what 2 Timothy 3:16 and other related verses in fact say. Among the many problematic consequences of these views is their inability to explain clearly why the canon of Scripture is closed. If God's action in and through some contemporary believers is not different in substance from his action in and through those whose writings formed part of Scripture, it is hard to see what firm theological reasons we have for not adding to Scripture 'inspiring' texts written subsequently.

A Spirit-given Scripture
What can be said further about the characteristics of a Scripture authored by God through the agency of the Spirit? The evangelical doctrine of inspiration has usually been explained as claiming the *plenary*, *verbal* inspiration of Scripture. 'Plenary' simply means 'full', and states that every part of Scripture has its origins in God.

---

42. See e.g. James Barr, *The Bible in the Modern World* (London: SCM, 1973); Paul J. Achtemeier, *The Inspiration of Scripture: Problems and Proposals* (Philadelphia: Westminster, 1980); William Abraham, *The Divine Inspiration of Holy Scripture* (Oxford: Oxford University Press, 1981).

43. Kern Robert Trembath, *Evangelical Theories of Biblical Inspiration: A Review and Proposal* (New York: Oxford University Press, 1987).

It is founded on the explicit biblical statement that '*all* Scripture is God-breathed'.

It is important to clarify what this claim does not entail, because both its proponents and its opponents have sometimes thought it says more than it in fact does. *Plenary* inspiration does not claim that every sentence in Scripture can be treated as a direct word from God direct to the individual. Because the whole of Scripture is breathed-out by God, every part needs to be interpreted in the light of its place in the history of salvation that Scripture unfolds, and in its literary context. Nor does plenary inspiration necessarily lead us to treat every part of Scripture as equally meaningful and significant. The four Gospels should be read and preached more often than the book of Esther, for example, because they are more closely related to the church's present life in Christ. To say this does not deny the plenary inspiration of Esther, but is rather to locate that book in the history of divine revelation and redemption.[44]

Verbal inspiration has been the focus of greater controversy in recent years. It has been at the heart of some sharp debates over the inerrancy and infallibility of Scripture, which will be discussed further in the following chapter. To speak of verbal inspiration is to say that Scripture's divine origin extends not just to its general message, but also to its individual words, and even to its letters, since often if a single letter is changed, the word is changed. In other words it was not that the Holy Spirit gave (e.g.) Isaiah the general idea of what he should write, leaving it to the prophet to fill out the details in words entirely of his own invention, like a secretary

---

44. On these two points, Bavinck says, 'Scripture may not be viewed atomistically as though every word and letter by itself is inspired by God as such and has its own meaning with its own infinite, divine content', and 'even the lowliest part has its place and meaning and at the same time is much farther removed from the centre than other parts' (*Reformed Dogmatics*, vol. 1, pp. 438–439). This being so, it has been perfectly consistent and workable in the past for the church to hold to a robust doctrine of Scripture even while debating the canonical status of certain books, since (by definition, in fact) no doctrines of significance are derived solely from such books.

composing a letter on the basis of a brief verbal outline given by the
boss. Such a scenario would require us to imagine that God gave the
Bible writers some basic clues, left them to their own devices, and
then was delighted to discover that out of their own resources they
had written exactly what he wanted to say. That assumes far greater
wisdom and knowledge of God in human beings, apart from divine
revelation, than the Bible leads us to expect to find. Instead verbal
inspiration claims that the Bible says *exactly* what God wants to say
because the Holy Spirit was responsible for every word written in
Scripture. He is the divine Author behind the human authors.

If this seems to express an unhealthy interest in tiny details of
Scripture, the reasonable response can be made that Christ himself
was similarly concerned with the jots and tittles of his Scriptures
(Matt. 5:17–18). Nevertheless the critics of verbal inspiration do
have a legitimate point to make, in that it is not individual words
that are the basic unit of meaning, but the speech act. (As we have
seen, speech acts can be as short as a phrase and as long as a book.)
It is indeed possible to change a letter, a word, or the structure of a
sentence without significantly altering the force and content of the
speech act performed by those words. The study of the history of
the transmission by copying of biblical manuscripts bears out this
point repeatedly. Some changes to even individual letters do change
the force and content of the speech act, but they certainly do not
do so in every case. It follows that, while 'verbal' inspiration is basically correct in what it affirms, its focus is not quite in the right
place. It is the *speech acts* of Scripture (its units of meaning: sentences, paragraphs and books) that have their origin in divine
authorship, because authors primarily author speech acts. The individual words *are* inspired (spoken out by God) to the extent that
they come together to express these speech acts. For, in Matthew
chapter 5, Jesus is interested in the jots and tittles of Scripture only
in that they serve to express the promises he has come to fulfil.[45]

---

45. Even when Calvin speaks of the Holy Spirit 'dictating' the words of
    Scripture, as he sometimes does, it is usually clear from the context that
    he has in mind not individual words as such, but the teaching those
    words express (e.g. Calvin, *Institutes* 4.8.8).

Divine action and human action in the writing of the Bible

It has previously been said that the Bible's focus in speaking of the Holy Spirit's work in relation to Scripture is to assert that God is active and humans are passive as regards the *origin* of Scripture. We have also seen that the Bible is relatively silent on the mode or mechanism by which the Spirit moved people to write Scripture. But we still need to ask what can be said reliably about this. Many evangelical writers in the past have spoken of the Bible writers as 'scribes' of the Holy Spirit, as God's 'pen-men', and as those to whom the Holy Spirit 'dictated' the words. The evangelical doctrine of inspiration is sometimes criticized at this point for (allegedly) proposing what its critics call 'mechanical' dictation. However, very few evangelicals have wanted to speak of the Bible writers as only passive, and not at all active in their own right in the writing of Scripture. Most have recognized that Scripture is as thoroughly human in character as it is divine. Bible writers clearly exhibit different styles and interests, as befits their character, gifts and background. The language of the Bible is ordinary human language; sometimes it is a work of high art, while at other times it is very down to earth. The Old Testament histories often refer to their use of other historical sources, and Luke introduces his Gospel by doing the same. The Bible is like any other book in this regard. Moreover our English translations have been produced through knowledge of the original languages, and in addition we rightly understand Scripture only by paying attention to the form of its literature and the historical contexts it describes and out of which it was written. To refuse to pay proper heed to any of these, out of a desire to defend the divine origin of Scripture, is in fact to denigrate Scripture by ignoring some fundamental features of the writings God has given us.

Therefore both the fully divine and fully human elements of Scripture must be taken into account, and not played off against each other. This means that, when we think about the relation of divine and human working together in the production of Scripture, it is clear that Scripture is an instance of God's providential activity. Throughout history God works through actions which his creatures have freely chosen in order to bring about the purposes he has decreed. People act freely, but not autonomously, under God's sovereignty. This principle surfaces explicitly in many places in Scripture, such as the selling of Joseph into slavery (Gen. 45:8), and supremely in the death of Christ (Acts 2:23). This is sometimes referred to, a little prosaically, as the 'concursive operation' of human and divine action. Warfield defines concursive operation thus: 'no human activity – not even the control of the will – is superseded, but the Holy Spirit works in, with and through them all in such a manner as to communicate to the product qualities distinctly superhuman'.[46] He applies the notion in detail to the production of Scripture thus: inspiration broadly defined, he says, refers to God's long-term preparation of the writer and his material. '[God] prepared a Paul to write, and the Paul he brought to the task was a Paul who spontaneously would write just such letters [as God intended Paul to write]'.[47] The Bible is thus entirely human and entirely divine, and God's action in producing it extends beyond the actual moment of writing, to cover the entirety of his providential work in the writers.

A number of people object to the doctrine of inspiration most strongly at this point. The last three centuries of biblical scholarship have given us significantly greater knowledge of the historical and cultural circumstances in which the Bible writers lived and worked than earlier generations possessed. It is argued that this has made the human aspect of Scripture loom larger, proportionally diminishing the divine aspect, and making it harder to propose a model of concursive operation of human and divine.[48] Warfield is especially critical of this argument, pointing out that, if our understanding of divine providence is properly in place, a greater recognition of the human element of Scripture need not diminish our acknowledgment of the divine element. Divine and human actions overlap here; they do not compete.[49] Behind many objections to the evangelical understanding of the action of the Holy Spirit in the authoring of Scripture lie objections to divine provi-

---

46. Warfield, *Inspiration and Authority*, p. 83.

47. Ibid., p. 155.

48. E.g. Bruce Vawter, *Biblical Inspiration* (London: Hutchison, 1972), p. 128.

49. A. N. S. Lane, 'B. B. Warfield on the Humanity of Scripture', *Vox evangelica* 16 (1986), pp. 77–94.

dence that lean more towards deism than they do towards a biblical doctrine of God, which states, however unfathomable it may ultimately be to us, that an action can be simultaneously an act of God and a genuinely human act.

The preservation of Scripture

10-6

The Holy Spirit and the transmission of Scripture

Once inspiration has been defined correctly as the action by the Holy Spirit of speaking directly through the *writers* of the Bible, it is clear that the Holy Spirit did not work in precisely the same way through those who *copied and transmitted* subsequent manuscripts of the Bible. Mistakes did occur in the copying of manuscripts, and the complex field of studies known as textual criticism has evolved to work with these manuscripts in order to determine the precise wording of the original manuscripts (usually known as the 'autographs'), which themselves have not to our knowledge been preserved. Thus it turns out that God providentially oversaw the naturally fallible process of the copying and transmission of the texts, with the result that those many texts which have been preserved make it possible, where they do differ from one another, to reconstruct the wording of the original with a very high degree of confidence in almost every case. Indeed the existence of God's Word in written, rather than simply oral, form made its preservation and transmission far more reliable. Whatever minor errors crept into the process of copying manuscripts, many of which can be sorted out by textual criticism, they are few in comparison to the modifications that happen to oral tradition over time. Although in some places in Scripture doubt still remains over the precise wording of the original text, no teaching of any significance depends on such a disputed text.

The previous discussion of verbal inspiration also sheds light on a question that arises here. Strictly speaking it is only the autographs, which we do not have, that are inspired. It is sometimes asked, then, not so much whether verbal inspiration is in error, but what practical value it has, since it is a statement directly about texts we do not have, and whose wording cannot be reconstructed with precision at every point. That makes verbal inspiration appear to some to be a purely hypothetical doctrine.

The answer commonly and rightly given to this is that no teaching of any significance depends on a text whose exact original form cannot confidently be reconstructed, and that in any case the large number of ancient Bible manuscripts in existence allows sophisticated decisions to be made about the wording of the original, far more reliably than with any other ancient text. To this we can also add that, since the primary focus of verbal inspiration is speech acts rather than words, and since the variations across the ancient manuscripts rarely raise doubt about the purpose and content of the speech act conveyed in a sentence or paragraph of the original, our texts come close enough to the original for verbal inspiration to be a meaningful doctrine that really does apply to the texts as we have them, and not a merely hypothetical doctrine.

The same point helps when thinking about the question of whether translations of the Bible can also be said, by extension, to be the inspired Word of God. It is of course the case that the words of the earthly Jesus as recorded in the New Testament are already translations into Greek of the Aramaic language he spoke. The words of Christ in our own language have therefore been doubly translated. (Only very rarely is a short phrase of Jesus' Aramaic words recorded, such as the words he spoke to Jairus' daughter to raise her from death, in Mark 5:41.) This observation has traditionally been expressed with two Latin phrases: we do not have Christ's *ipsissima verba* (his very words), but we do have his *ipsissima vox* (his very message – or, in the terms I am using, his actual speech acts). This can lead Christians to be concerned that our contemporary Bibles give us access to Christ's words only through a glass darkly, because translation necessarily muddies the waters. Now of course those who have learned the original languages can sometimes teach us things about the meaning of a text that our English translations cannot or do not make clear. Yet if we keep in mind that the focus of the Holy Spirit's act of inspiration was the speech acts, then we can be confident that these have been accurately translated, whatever questions there may be about the translation of individual words from one language to another. It is this observation that points to the virtues of what are normally called 'dynamic equivalence' translations of the Bible, such as the New International family of versions. They are based on the quite correct notion that the basic unit of meaning is the speech act (such as the sentence or phrase), and that this, rather than the individual word, is the unit the translator needs to concentrate on reproducing in the receptor language.[50]

The Holy Spirit and the canon of Scripture

The Spirit was also at work in the early centuries of the church in the compilation of the canon of Scripture. The history of this process has been written in detail many times. In very simple terms, it comprised the remarkably rapid and widespread recognition of at least the four Gospels and of a number of Paul's letters as Scripture (the latter witnessed to very early in 2 Pet. 3:15–16),

---

50. Of course, though, every good translation practises a mixture of 'dynamic equivalence' and 'word for word' translation. Despite the claims that the publishers and editorial boards of new English translations sometimes make for their work, all good translations focus primarily on reproducing the 'thought' (i.e. the speech act) of the original, while reflecting the sentence structure and vocabulary choice of the original as far as the constraints of the receptor language allow. To give an example: what largely distinguishes the recent English Standard Version from the New International Version, and against which many have pitted it, is only the greater willingness of the ESV translators to sacrifice naturalness of expression in English, in order to follow as closely as possible the Greek sentence structure. It is certainly not a virtue in translation to be content only to translate the overall 'thought', without striving to reflect as much as possible of the structure and vocabulary usage of the original. Yet neither ought a translation to be praised too highly if it regularly turns Greek sentences, which would have sounded quite natural to a Greek-speaking audience, into stilted bits of English no native speaker of the language would ever utter, simply in order to reflect details in the original that may well not be meaning bearing in any case, but are simply features of Greek linguistic style. There is, in other words, more than one kind of accuracy in translation, and every translation constantly has to make a choice about where to make sacrifices.

and an extended period in which uncertainty lingered in some areas over other books, such as Jude and Revelation.

The most significant element distinguishing a Protestant understanding of this process from a Roman Catholic one relates to the nature of the action of the Holy Spirit thought to lie behind the history. For Catholicism, the Spirit was primarily at work in and through the church in an essentially new way, evolving for the church its authority to determine the content of Scripture. Over the centuries this developed into the authority of the teaching office of the structured church to determine the meaning of Scripture. For Protestants, by contrast, the Spirit's work in the historical events of the compilation of the canon did not constitute the creation of a new reality and authority in the church. It was, rather, an act in service of his original authorship of Scripture, by which he brought the church, through a complex historical process, to recognize which books he had in fact authored and which he had not. The lists of canonical books which leaders in the early church occasionally issued were thus not so much attempts by church authorities to impose order on a confused situation, but were rather statements of what the church as a whole was finding to be the case with Scripture. Through the Spirit the church therefore did not create the canon of Scripture, but came to recognize it. This is an aspect of God's faithfulness to and consistency with his Word, bringing about human recognition of what he has already performed in the breathing out of Scripture.

The illumination of Scripture

On the basis of such passages as 1 Corinthians 2:6–16 and 2 Corinthians 3:12 – 4:6 has been developed a description of what is called the illumination of Scripture by the Holy Spirit. This refers to the fact that it is only by the Holy Spirit opening our hearts and minds to his words in Scripture that we come to accept Scripture as the Word of God, to understand it and trust it. A typical statement from the post-Reformation period of the Reformed view of illumination and its relation to the role of the church is found in Francis Turretin, one of the most influential Reformed theologians of the seventeenth century. He says that the Bible itself, with its remarkable characteristics and content, is the argument on account of which he believes; the Holy Spirit is the efficient cause and principle that induces him to believe; and the church is the instrument and means through which he comes to believe.[51] Thus, while both the church's testimony and the Bible itself are means God uses to bring us to himself, the actual power that brings us to saving faith in the Lord is the Holy Spirit.

Crucial to the Reformers' view of this action of the Spirit is that his illuminating work took place not through the church but through Scripture. Calvin makes the point this way: 'the Word is the instrument by which the Lord dispenses the illumination of his Spirit to believers. For they know no other Spirit than him who dwelt and spoke in the apostles.'[52] Similarly, but less dynamically, from Turretin just over a century later, speaking of Word and Spirit: 'The former works objectively, the latter efficiently; the former strikes the ears from without, the latter opens the heart from within.'[53]

This was an argument directed in three directions at once. Negatively against *Roman Catholicism*, it asserted that the Spirit required the church only as an instrument, not as the actual dynamic, by which people came to faith. Negatively against the sixteenth-century *Radical Reformation*, it asserted that the Spirit regularly illumined minds through the content of the written Word, not by providing revelations to the individual apart from or despite Scripture. And *positively*, it served to demonstrate the faithfulness and consistency of God in revelation. God had spoken words in human language, and had identified himself with the speech acts performed by means of those words. The result of this was that human beings, who can have no reliable saving knowledge of God or access to him either through their own powers or through anything in the world around them, could confidently trust in God as the covenant-making God he revealed himself to be. Now that those words from God had been written in Scripture, God, through the person of the Spirit, would stand

---

51. Turretin, *Elenctic Theology* 2.6.6.

52. Calvin, *Institutes* 1.9.3.

53. Turretin, *Elenctic Theology* 2.2.9.

by them and remain faithful to them wherever Scripture was read and preached. The Spirit acts to minister the meaning of the words of Scripture, not to manipulate or modify it. (There will be more to say about all of this when we examine 'Scripture and the Christian community' in chapter 5.)

The doctrine of the illumination of Scripture by the Holy Spirit is usually defended as the only means by which the authority of Scripture can be made to rest, as it must rest, on God himself alone. It is not that the character of Scripture as the Word of God lacks external evidence, such as might be found in its history and in its content. Yet these, according to Calvin, although they are 'very useful aids', come in only once the certainty of Scripture as the Word of God has been fixed in our minds by the Holy Spirit.[54] However, it is also evident that illumination is not just arrived at by logical deduction, but is a natural outworking of the character and actions of God, as we saw them in the biblical outline of the previous chapter. Having spoken the words of his covenant, and having caused them to be written, God continues to show himself as Lord by being also the servant Lord, who faithfully speaks again his covenant promise in truth and power, bringing knowledge of himself through that promise. God is in Scripture in the sense that the speech acts of Scripture are an aspect of his active presence; it is then quite natural that the ongoing illuminatory work of the Holy Spirit should occur in and through those words.

Summary

I have previously given a biblical outline of Scripture's nature and function as God's words, describing Scripture as an aspect of God in action in his world. This chapter has given theological expression to that remarkably close relationship of Scripture to God's

---

54. Calvin, *Institutes* 1.8.1. The rational verification of Scripture by external evidence, while never eclipsing the internal testimony of the Spirit, regularly became more prominent in Reformed theology as it developed from the sixteenth through to the twentieth century.

activity, by relating Scripture in turn to the Father, the Son and the Spirit. It should be clear that the view of Scripture I have been outlining cannot be treated as merely the preface to the real meat of the doctrines of God, Christ, Spirit and salvation. Rather, when properly understood, the doctrine of Scripture is thoroughly woven into a biblical doctrine of the Trinity. We cannot properly describe the actions of the triune God in redemption and revelation without tying Scripture to God as a key part of his redemptive and revelatory activity, since that is precisely what he himself has done. And this consequently ties the speech acts of Scripture directly to God himself. In this sense the doctrine of Scripture ought to be a subsection within our doctrines of God, of redemption and of revelation.

Whenever we encounter the speech acts of Scripture, we encounter God himself in action. The Father presents himself to us as a God who makes and keeps his covenant promises. The Son comes to us as the Word of God, knowable to us through his words. The Spirit ministers these words to us, illuminating our minds and hearts, so that in receiving, understanding and trusting them, we receive, know and trust God himself.

4. THE ATTRIBUTES OF SCRIPTURE:
   A DOCTRINAL OUTLINE

It has been common for evangelical writing on the doctrine of Scripture to outline the doctrine under a series of headings, usually termed the 'attributes' of Scripture. *Necessity, sufficiency, clarity* and *authority* have historically been the attributes most commonly cited. In this book I have wanted to move towards these same headings, because they are truthful and significant, and therefore ought to remain fundamental to our beliefs about Scripture. But I have also wanted to take a route towards them that has not always been explicitly taken, that is, through the biblical and theological outlines of the previous two chapters.

Of course a great deal of careful biblical and theological thought lay behind the development of these common doctrinal statements about Scripture's attributes. Yet it often happens in the history of theological thought that a doctrinal statement is picked up, passed on, rejected by some and defended by others, offered as a rallying cry for the orthodox against the unorthodox, and in the process loses in many people's minds its biblical and theological underpinnings. This has two unfortunate effects. First, it becomes rather easy for the doctrine's opponents to portray it as a doctrine with roots more in the features of human cultures and philosophies than in Christian faith, and thereby to claim that it is not an essential component of Christian belief and teaching. Secondly, the doctrine's defenders can find themselves establishing their identity on a doctrine whose rich basis in Scripture and theology they take for granted, without being able to articulate it in a satisfactory way. One danger then always lurks: that the doctrine will gradually lose its proper biblical shape, and will begin to distort biblical teaching, rather than properly propound it. Evangelical enthusiasm for systematic theology sometimes blinds people to this danger. Others are wary of systematics precisely because they recognize very clearly the dangers of only ever reading Scripture through the grid of an inflexible theological system. I have attempted to allow a sensitivity to this concern to shape this book.

This chapter retains the traditional evangelical doctrinal headings for Scripture, because I remain convinced that they are still excellent headings under which to express faithful Christian thought about Scripture in doctrinal form. However, the biblical and theological outlines of the previous two chapters will allow us to affirm and clarify both what is implied by each of these doctrinal headings, and what is not implied, building them firmly on explicit foundations. Too often these different doctrines of Scripture have been extended in the heat of debate beyond what can justifiably be claimed for them. That has been done many times since the Reformation. It has been done by evangelical believers who were nervous that the doctrine was under attack and rightly wanted to shore it up as firmly as possible. It has also been done by opponents, who either deliberately or accidentally outlined an overextended caricature of the doctrine, which was then easy to dismiss as wrong or silly. All doctrinal statements arise out of the need to refute teachings believed to be false. That is, they are shaped with apologetic and polemical intent. Taking note of the purpose each doctrine serves will enable us to see how each one can continue to be a useful sharp-edged tool in modern Christian life and thought.

The necessity of Scripture

It has been common in evangelical writing on Scripture to say that, first of all, Scripture is *necessary*. This may not be the first attribute many evangelicals today would offer as a description of Scripture, but nevertheless it has been a significant one in evangelical theology. As with many aspects of Protestant theology, the doctrine was stated plainly by the early Reformers, and then described in more systematic form by theologians in the subsequent two centuries.

The best-known example of the former is found in John Calvin, right at the beginning of his *Institutes of the Christian Religion*. Under the heading 'Scripture is needed as guide and teacher for anyone who would come to God the creator' Calvin famously draws an analogy between the necessity of Scripture and the need for spectacles to correct the vision of those with poor eyesight:

> Just as old or bleary-eyed men and those with weak vision, if you thrust before them a most beautiful volume, even if they recognise it to be some sort of writing, yet can scarcely construe two words, but with the aid of spectacles will begin to read distinctly; so Scripture, gathering up the otherwise confused knowledge of God in our minds, having dispersed our dullness, clearly shows us the true God. (*Institutes* 1.6.1)

Calvin has in mind here God's revelation of his reality and glory as the creator through the physical creation (analogous to the 'most beautiful volume' in this quotation), of which God speaks in Romans 1:19–20. However, that revelation in itself has no saving benefit for humanity, because in our sinfulness we suppress the knowledge of the creator to which it should lead us (Rom. 1:18). For Calvin, the fall did not entirely erase human knowledge of God, and consequently Scripture can serve as the necessary lens for putting into focus for us knowledge of God which is already there, but which without God's word to us in Scripture is seriously blurred by our sinful perspective.

Calvin then adds further reasons for asserting the necessity of Scripture. By revealing himself in words, whether those words came through oracles and visions or through what Calvin calls 'the ministry of men', God 'rendered faith unambiguous forever, a faith that should be superior to all opinion' (*Institutes* 1.6.2). At this point Calvin is thinking of revelation as verbal, but not necessarily in written form. His point seems to be that it is the verbal form of revelation which allows it to be considered and understood in such a way that it can be reliably known to have come from God. It is thus different from a non-verbal revelation in the form purely of a feeling, say, or of an emotional state. Such non-verbal revelation could not be adequately described in words by its recipient, either to herself or to another. It could not therefore stand as demonstrably divine revelation.

This kind of statement on Scripture argues that we must identify Scripture as the necessary Word of God because without such a Word our knowledge of God would be insufficiently grounded, unreliable and even (we might say) too subjective.

Sentiments like this were expressed increasingly strongly in the three centuries following the Reformation, and have been subjected to the searching criticism that they owe far more to the Enlightenment's desire to rest the certainty of knowledge on principles that can be derived from human reason acting autonomously than they do to any convictions that can reasonably be said to be Christian and biblical. After all, it is asked, is Christian faith not more to do with walking by faith than by sight? Is a belief in the necessity of Scripture, some will allege, not in the end a doctrine produced by people who are temperamentally unable to live with uncertainty in life?

There is no need to defend post-Reformation theologians against every charge of becoming too rationalistic in their understanding of the certainty of faith, for such rationalism is certainly evident in some of their writings. However, what has rarely been pointed out is that not only Calvin, but also many of his theological heirs, were primarily concerned with believers' *assurance* that their knowledge of God is knowledge of the true God, and not of an idol, and therefore that their relationship with God was genuine and not a fantasy or a sham. This is the focus of the doctrine of the necessity of Scripture. It does not represent an attempt to establish Christian faith as a belief that meets the philosophical standards set by a supposedly autonomous human reason.

Indeed Scripture speaks regularly of a right kind of certainty in faith, which is not some philosophical certainty, but is instead an assurance of and confidence in the genuineness of our knowledge of God, and of our relationship with him. For example, John's first letter was written with the express intention 'that you may know that you have eternal life' (1 John 5:13). Luke's entire Gospel was written so that Theophilus 'may know the certainty of the things you have been taught' (Luke 1:4), which unquestionably speaks of the importance of reliable knowledge of certain facts about Jesus Christ. In the light of these statements by biblical authors about their intentions in writing, it must be judged that too many commentators have been too quick to accuse evangelical theologians of obsession with philosophical certainty of a very Western kind, when what they have primarily had in mind has been assurance of the reality of relationship with God.

Back in Calvin's exposition of necessity, he then moves to the necessity of the *written form* of divine verbal revelation. This form was necessary 'in order that the truth might abide forever in the world with a continuous succession of teaching and survive through all ages' (*Institutes* 1.6.2). A carefully copied text is likely to undergo fewer changes and corruptions, both accidental and deliberate, than a body of purely oral tradition. As Calvin summarizes it, a written revelation was necessary to ensure that God's revelation 'should neither perish through forgetfulness nor vanish through error nor be corrupted by the audacity of men' (*Institutes* 1.6.3).

These latter reasons have not been simply deduced by Calvin from the fact of revelation having written form, but can be found on occasion expressed in Scripture itself. After the defeat of the Amalekites by Joshua, the Lord said to Moses, 'Write this on a scroll as something to be remembered and make sure that Joshua hears it, because I will completely blot out the name of Amalek from under heaven' (Exod. 17:14). The writing down of the acts of God here is commanded by God to make it easier for his people to be reminded of the completeness of his victory over their enemies, and therefore of his faithfulness to his covenant with them. Elsewhere God instructs Ezekiel regarding the design of the temple and its regulations and laws: 'Write these down before them [the people of Israel] so that they may be faithful to its design and follow all its regulations' (Ezek. 43:11). God knows it is easier to be faithful to written commands, rather than merely spoken ones.

It is noteworthy that Francis Turretin, the Genevan theologian writing just over a century after Calvin, adds very little of substance to Calvin's doctrine of necessity. The two main developments are that he, typically, presents the teaching in more systematic fashion, and additionally responds to a number of detailed objections subsequently made against the doctrine, primarily by Roman Catholics. More clearly than Calvin, Turretin distinguishes the question of the necessity of Scripture into the need, first, for a verbal revelation, and secondly for a written form for that verbal revelation. His understanding of the function of Scripture is remarkably dynamic: 'It is the "seed" of which we are born again (1 Pet. 1:23), the "light" by which we are directed (Ps. 119:105), the "food" upon which we feed (Heb. 5:13, 14) and the "foundation" upon which we are built (Eph. 2:20)' (*Elenctic Theology* 2.1.1). He agrees with Calvin that a verbal revelation is required to lead us to salvation, and that this is because our sinfulness blinds us to God's self-revelation through creation. He strongly emphasizes the sheer limitations of revelation through creation: 'Indeed, it [natural revelation] shows that God exists, and of what nature, both in unity of essence and as possessed of different attributes, but does not tell us who he is individually and with regard to persons' (*Elenctic Theology* 2.1.6).

Thus a *verbal* revelation is absolutely necessary if humanity is to know God as he truly is, and to be able to enter into a saving knowledge of God. Turretin, like many post-Reformation theologians, clarifies that *written* revelation is, by contrast, not *absolutely* necessary. This is so because there have been times in history, such as before the time of Moses, when some people did indeed have saving knowledge of God, but without written revelation. Written Scripture is therefore necessary only in the sense that God has now given us a written revelation and thereby decreed that it is necessary for us. God could have continued to reveal himself to us through visions, spoken oracles, dreams and so on. However, he has chosen that his primary self-revelation not be in this form, but written for us in the Bible. Turretin puts it this way: 'God indeed was not bound to the Scriptures, but he has bound us to them' (*Elenctic Theology* 2.2.2). Herman Bavinck links the necessity of Scripture directly to the fact that divine revelation has come to a climax in Christ.[1]

Turretin's points are directed most immediately against Roman Catholics who would deny the necessity of written revelation, 'in order', as he says, 'the more easily to establish their unwritten traditions and the supreme tribunal of the pope himself' (*Elenctic Theology* 2.2.1). This makes evident the fact that the doctrine of the necessity of Scripture is less a detailed subpoint of some logically constructed doctrinal scheme, and more akin to an additional perspective from which the fundamental theological insights of the Protestant Reformation can be articulated. It so happened that 'the necessity of Scripture' did not grow to be regarded as one of the Reformation's great summarizing watchwords, as *sola scriptura* (Scripture alone) did. Nevertheless necessity sits right at the heart of the ways in which *sola scriptura* is explicated and defended. If Scripture alone is claimed to be the supreme authority in Christian thinking and living, that is because both its content (the verbal revelation) and its form (the written Scriptures) are indispensable. (*Sola scriptura* will be dealt with more fully in the next chapter.)

Turretin ends his defence of the necessity of a written Scripture by adding two things. Similarly to Calvin he argues that a written Scripture is necessary for the preservation of the word, and also for its propagation. He notes that written communication was the normal means by which sovereigns ensured the faithful preservation and propagation of their laws (*Elenctic Theology* 2.2.6). Other post-Reformation theologians mentioned Jude 3 at this point, which expresses the way in which writing followed naturally from the nature of the role of apostles as universal teachers.[2]

---

1. Herman Bavinck, *Reformed Dogmatics*, vol. 1, *Prolegomena*, gen. ed. John Bolt, tr. John Vriend (Grand Rapids: Baker Academic, 2003), p. 471.

2. See Richard A. Muller, *Post-Reformation Reformed Dogmatics*, vol. 2, *Holy Scripture: The Cognitive Foundation of Theology* (Grand Rapids: Baker, 1993), pp. 172–173.

Turretin also responds to some objections to the stress on the necessity of written revelation. First, some churches may have existed for a time without the written word of God, he acknowledges, but points out that they could not have come into existence without the verbal message of Scripture being passed on to them orally. Nor is it true that Christ's statement that 'you are not to be called "Rabbi", for you have only one Master and you are all brothers' (Matt. 23:8) excludes Scripture. For here Christ is not setting himself in opposition to Scripture, through which he now addresses us, but to the Pharisees who had established a false authority of their own (*Elenctic Theology* 2.2.12).

Secondly, says Turretin, the Bible's references to believers being taught directly by the Holy Spirit, and needing no other teacher (e.g. Jer. 31:34; 1 John 2:27) do not make Scripture less necessary. Rather 'The Spirit is the teacher; Scripture is the doctrine which he teaches us.' This point, seemingly directed against some parts of the radical wing of the Reformation, argues that the ministry of teachers of Scripture will end only in heaven, for it is only then that 'each one will see God as he is face to face' (*Elenctic Theology* 2.2.9). Thus the promise of Jeremiah 31:34 has not yet been entirely fulfilled. This point remains a vital one in the contemporary church. Both announcements by ordained church leaders and statements by people judged by themselves or others to be especially anointed by the Spirit can come to be treated in practice as on an equal footing with Scripture as the 'word of God'. This remains the case whether it is a pope speaking *ex cathedra*, an acknowledged prophet predicting the future (the most notorious examples), or even (more subtly) an evangelical pastor who in effect commands members of his congregation to believe things or do things that cannot be substantiated by Scripture. The evangelical doctrine of Scripture is therefore an outcry against Roman Catholic understandings of revelation, and against any practice that effectively regards the as yet unfulfilled predictions about the future made by a contemporary prophet as equally authoritative as God's words in Scripture. It is equally a warning against any evangelical pastor exercising an authority that has come to rest in himself, rather than residing (where it should do) in the action of the Holy Spirit pressing the meaning of Scripture on to the hearts and minds of those whom he teaches.

To these two accounts of the necessity of Scripture from Calvin and Turretin I want to add something assumed by both and sometimes referred to, but not stated explicitly, as the basis on which the doctrine is built. Turretin states, as we saw, that natural revelation alone can reveal God's existence and nature, but not *who* he is; it is here that we find the most profound basis for expounding a doctrine of the necessity of Scripture. The whole pattern of God's self-revelation is that he establishes a covenant relationship between himself and his people, and this is a relationship in which he makes himself known. He does not reveal himself exhaustively, but the God he shows himself to be in his covenant relationship is the God he really is. The very nature of God as a being who is himself three persons in relation, who chooses to open those relationships out in order to relate to others, requires that his revelation be verbal. His relationship with us would simply not be the kind of relationship he in fact has chosen to establish, if it were established and sustained without words. The reality of the Trinity, and the purpose of the incarnation, crucifixion, resurrection and ascension are sufficiently complex that they cannot be mimed, or communicated through a religious impulse or sensation; they need to be spoken. One of the aims of the previous two chapters of this book is to establish this.

Turning specifically to the *writtenness* of Scripture, this aspect of divine revelation is strongly implied by the covenantal nature of God's plan and purposes for human salvation. Turretin appealed to the fact that kings and princes normally have their laws written down, to ensure their permanence and ease of propagation. And I have noted in a previous chapter the similarities between parts of Scripture and ancient treaties agreed by an overlord with his new subjects, and also how the New Testament makes clear that Christ, whose word is brought to us in the New Testament, is in himself and in his words the fulfilment of the old covenant. On this basis I called Scripture 'the book of the covenant'. It is in line with the very nature of the covenant that God has established and revealed progressively through time that its stipulations and history, as a witness to God's faithfulness to it, be written down. It was not an absolute necessity that it was, but it is highly appropriate to the nature of his chosen form of revelation and salvation that God ensured it was.[3]

A final and different point can be made about the necessity of written revelation, in the context of contemporary thought about language and writing. A variety of thinkers in the twentieth century, albeit in different ways, cast doubt on the stability of the meaning of written language, in contrast to face-to-face speech. The philosopher Paul Ricoeur argued that reading a text 'is not a relation of interlocution, not an instance of dialogue'.[4] What a speaker is *doing* by the words he utters (what speech-act theorists call the 'illocutionary force' of his speech act, such as warning, promising etc.) is often communicated in spoken discourse through non-verbal means such as gesture, and these are of course lacking in the case of written language. Thus, concludes Ricoeur, 'the illocutionary force is less inscribable than the propositional meaning'.[5] The influential German philosopher Hans-Georg Gadamer made similar statements in the middle of the twentieth century.[6] If this were to be universally true, then the problem for Scripture would be serious, since its overall illocutionary force of covenant-making is fundamental to its very nature as a covenant book.

The most helpful response to this from a Christian theologian, for our purposes, has come from Kevin Vanhoozer. He has argued

---

3. Bavinck compellingly holds together Scripture as the record of God's revelation in history and as the present voice of the living God: '[Scripture] is rooted in a centuries-long history and is the fruit of God's revelation among the people of Israel and in Christ . . . [but also] In it God daily comes to his people . . . It does not just tie us to the past; it binds us to the living Lord in the heavens' (Bavinck, *Reformed Dogmatics*, vol. 1, pp. 384–385).

4. Paul Ricoeur, *Hermeneutics and the Human Sciences: Essays on Language, Action and Interpretation*, ed. and tr. John B. Thompson (Cambridge: Cambridge University Press, 1981), p. 146.

5. Paul Ricoeur, *Interpretation Theory: Discourse and the Surplus of Meaning* (Fort Worth: Texas Christian University Press, 1976), p. 27.

6. Hans-Georg Gadamer, *Truth and Method*, 2nd rev. ed., tr. and rev. Joel Weinsheimer and Donald G. Marshall (New York: Crossroad, 1990), pp. 392–395.

that the *genres* of literary texts (e.g. that a piece of writing is a narrative, prophecy or apocalyptic) make up for the elements of
face-to-face communication that the situation of reading, or listening to the reading of, a written text lacks. 'The concept of genre
. . . describes the illocutionary act at the level of the whole' is how
he puts it.[7] The situation of reading a text may give no opportunity
to see the author's gestures and facial expressions, but writing does
have the ability to communicate the nature of the act of communication the author was performing. It does so through *literary*
means, as the illocutionary force is conveyed through different literary genres. For example, the beginning of the Gospel of Luke
tells us that what we are reading is a kind of history; the beginning
of the book of Revelation signals that this will be apocalyptic
writing; and so on. Thus the doctrine of the necessity of a *written*
revelation does not force us to conclude philosophically that we
are automatically condemned, as Bible readers, to being further
distanced from God because he speaks to us through a text rather
than through a vision or dream. Nor does it entail the conclusion
that we can be less certain about the meaning of God's communication to us, just because it comes through a text and not through
direct speech of some kind.

The sufficiency of Scripture

Before discussing what I am calling here the sufficiency of
Scripture, it must be noted that there is nothing fixed about the
terms used to describe these doctrines of Scripture. None is a
term given to us in Scripture, so we are not bound to them. It is
the concept to which each refers that is important, not the term.
The use of the term 'sufficiency' has been especially fluid. Thus
Francis Turretin in the seventeenth century does not use the term
as a general heading, preferring instead to speak of 'the perfection
of the Scriptures' (*Elenctic Theology* 1.16). To repeat: although uses

---

7. Kevin J. Vanhoozer, *Is There a Meaning in This Text? The Bible, the Reader
and the Morality of Literary Knowledge* (Leicester: Apollos, 1998), p. 341.

of the terminology have varied, the concepts referred to by these differing terms have been widely accepted by most Christians across the centuries.

The claim that the Bible is 'sufficient', says one writer, 'is the dominating tone for the entire chorus of the church'.[8] It rests on those many parts of Scripture that speak of a completeness in God's law and word. Thus Psalm 119:1 assumes God's law communicates everything a person needs to know to live a blameless life:

> Blessed are those whose ways are blameless
> who walk according to the law of the Lord.

Paul speaks in 2 Timothy 3:15 of the Scriptures as 'able to make you wise for salvation through faith in Jesus Christ', referring in his immediate context primarily to the way in which the Old Testament is a complete witness to and preparation for faith in Jesus Christ. The closing section of the book of Revelation promises a divine curse for anyone who adds to or subtracts from its words (Rev. 22:18–19). These words, when placed not just at the end of the Apocalypse but also subsequently at the end of the New Testament canon, and immediately followed not by the expectation of further verbal revelation from God but only now the coming again of Jesus Christ (v. 20), look back over the whole of Scripture and imply that it is now complete.

The confession that Scripture as divine revelation is sufficient for knowledge of salvation and godly living was commonly made in the early centuries of the church. Athanasius, bishop of Alexandria in the fourth century, wrote that 'the sacred and divinely inspired Scriptures are sufficient for the exposition of the truth'.[9] For Augustine, some eighty years later, 'among the things that are plainly laid down in Scripture are to be found all matters

---

8. G. C. Berkouwer, *Holy Scripture*, tr. and ed. Jack B. Rogers (Grand Rapids: Eerdmans, 1975), p. 305.

9. Athanasius, *Against the Pagans* 1, Nicene and Post-Nicene Fathers, vol. 4, ed. Philip Schaff and Henry Wace (Grand Rapids: Eerdmans, 1957).

that concern faith and the manner of life – to wit, hope and love'.[10] This conviction that Scripture contains everything needed for Christian faith and life is sometimes known as the 'material' sufficiency of Scripture. It lasted relatively unchanged, although some of the fathers of the early church did express themselves in two ways that, over the centuries, would grow to threaten a healthy outworking of belief in the sufficiency of Scripture. First, there was a growing acceptance of what were taken to be apostolic traditions passed down in ways other than by Scripture. Basil of Caesarea referred to these in the fourth century; he had in mind such practices as the use of the sign of the cross at baptism and facing east to pray.[11] Secondly, the ability of Scripture to be its own interpreter was called into question. This is sometimes called the 'formal' sufficiency of Scripture (in contrast to 'material' sufficiency), and is very close to the idea of the clarity of Scripture. This tendency began for very understandable reasons, when it was necessary to deal with those groups who were becoming heretical not by appealing to other sources than Scripture, but by misinterpreting Scripture itself (e.g. arguing that Jesus was not fully equal in divinity with the Father). Church tradition was appealed to, not as a second authority alongside Scripture, but in order to reinforce the true message of Scripture.[12]

Through the Middle Ages the predominant view was that Scripture was sufficient on matters relating directly to salvation. As

---

10. Augustine, *On Christian Doctrine* 2.9, Nicene and Post-Nicene Fathers, vol. 2, ed. Philip Schaff (Grand Rapids: Eerdmans, 1956).

11. Basil of Caesarea, *Concerning the Holy Spirit* 66, Nicene and Post-Nicene Fathers, vol. 8, ed. Philip Schaff and Henry Wace (Grand Rapids: Eerdmans, n. d.).

12. The most widely quoted example of this tendency is from Vincent of Lérins, in the fifth century: 'Since the canon of Scripture is complete, and is abundantly sufficient for every purpose, what need is there to add to it the authority of the church's interpretation? The reason is, of course, that by its very depth the Holy Scripture is not received by all in one and the same sense, . . . [so that] we can find almost as many interpretations as there are men.' So how is the right interpretation to be

the most influential theologian of the period, Thomas Aquinas, put it, 'The truth of faith is sufficiently plain in the teaching of Christ and the Apostles.'[13] Yet two views were growing: that apostolic material on issues of church practice was passed down over time separately from Scripture, either orally or through customary practice, and also that the definitive voice on the interpretation of Scripture was not the Spirit speaking through Scripture itself, but was the Spirit speaking through the increasingly authoritative ecclesiastical centre in Rome. When these non-biblical and supposedly apostolic church practices came increasingly to impinge on areas relating directly to salvation, as they did, then the material sufficiency of Scripture was effectively denied.

At the heart of the Protestant Reformation in the early part of the sixteenth century was the strong reassertion of the doctrine of the sufficiency of Scripture. The First Helvetic Confession of 1536 provides a typical example of this renewed commitment to a full outworking in church life of the material sufficiency of Scripture: 'Biblical Scripture . . . alone deals with everything that serves the true knowledge, love and honour of God, as well as true piety and the making of a godly, honest and blessed life.' Article 6 of the Church of England's Thirty-Nine Articles is similar: 'Holy Scripture containeth all things necessary to salvation: so that whatsoever is not read therein, nor may be proved thereby, is not to be required of any man, that it should be believed as an article of the Faith, or be thought requisite or necessary to salvation.' The influential Second Helvetic Confession of 1566, which came, as largely did the First, from the pen of Heinrich Bullinger of the church in Zurich, goes a step further in specifying that Scripture's sufficiency extends as far as allowing us

---

reached? Says Vincent, 'in the catholic church itself especial care must be taken that we hold to that which has been believed everywhere, always and by all men. For that is truly and rightly "catholic"' (Vincent of Lérins, 'The Commonitory', in *Early Medieval Theology*, Library of Christian Classics, vol. 9, tr. and ed. George E. McCracken and Allen Cabaniss [London: SCM, 1957], p 38).

13. Aquinas, *Summa Theologiae* (London: Blackfriars, 1964), 2.2 q.1 a.10.

to derive from it 'the reformation and government of churches'. A particularly distinguishing feature of the Reformation was its insistence on the formal sufficiency of Scripture. Calvin states it thus: 'the highest proof of Scripture derives in general from the fact that God in person speaks in it'.[14] For the Reformers, Scripture not only sufficiently contained everything necessary for knowledge of salvation and godly living, but it also received its authority not from any individual or church institution, but from God alone as he spoke through Scripture, in a manner sufficient for our acceptance of it.

When the sufficiency of Scripture is expressed in these terms, it is evident that theologians of the Reformation expounded sufficiency to make a point against opponents on both sides. Against Roman Catholics they were denying that it is primarily through the official teaching institution of the church in Rome that the Holy Spirit speaks in order to give Scripture its authority. Against the Anabaptists of the Radical Reformation they were denying that Scripture's authority derives from the use of it by certain individuals claiming to be specially endowed with the Spirit. In fact these two apparently very different positions, Roman and Radical, were making the same basic mistake of effectively subjecting Scripture to the authority of certain individuals. Instead, the Reformers insisted, the Scripture the Holy Spirit authored in the past receives its authority in the present from the fact that God the Holy Spirit continues to speak in it and through it the same message he once uttered.

The relationship between Scripture and Spirit is made particularly clear in Calvin's reply to Cardinal Jacopo Sadoleto, Archbishop of Carpentras, who had written a letter in which he called the city of Geneva back into the Roman fold: 'seeing how dangerous it would be to boast of the Spirit without the Word,' argued Calvin, '[God] declared that the Church is indeed governed by the Holy Spirit, but in order that the government might not be

---

14. John Calvin, *Institutes of the Christian Religion*, Library of Christian Classics, vols. 20–21, ed. John T. McNeill, tr. Ford Lewis Battles (Philadelphia: Westminster, 1960), 1.7.4.

vague or unstable, he annexed it to the Word'. Calvin lumps the
pope and the Anabaptists together, accusing both of glorying in
the Spirit in a way that tends 'to sink and bury the Word of God'.[15]
Indeed in subsequent centuries other seemingly different movements within Christianity have in effect done the same thing as
Rome and the Anabaptists. Rationalists such as Spinoza located
the working of the Spirit in the human mind and conscience. The
influential theologian Friedrich Schleiermacher located it in the
religious community's sense of dependence on God. The effects
of each of these approaches are still felt, and all have in common
the separation of Spirit from Word: the search for the guiding of
the Spirit not in and through Scripture, but in some supposedly
special individuals, or in some universal aspect of humanity. The
consequence of this is always a failure to confess the sufficiency of
Scripture.

As we continue to formulate and explain the sufficiency of
Scripture, as we must, this polemical context in which it reached
full expression cannot be ignored. If it is ignored, then the doctrine will be distorted into claiming something different, and
usually something extended beyond what can properly be
claimed. It should be clearly noted here that the key issue at stake
in the Protestant doctrine of the sufficiency of Scripture is
the nature of the Holy Spirit's ongoing activity in relation to
Scripture. It should not be thought that lengthy discussion of
these doctrinal attributes of Scripture in some way exalts 'Word'
over 'Spirit'. Instead underlying all discussion of these scriptural
attributes is the conviction that the Spirit is thoroughly at work in
and through Scripture, and that his work needs to be properly
outlined and acknowledged. One might even say that these
Protestant doctrines of the Word are in fact aspects of the doctrine of the work of the Holy Spirit.

In the century or two following the Reformation, the fullest
and most mature confessional statement on the sufficiency

---

15. John Calvin and Jacopo Sadoleto, *A Reformation Debate: Sadoleto's Letter to
the Genevans and Calvin's Reply*, ed. John C. Olin (New York: Harper &
Row, 1966), p. 60.

of Scripture is found in the Westminster Confession of Faith (1646):

> The whole counsel of God concerning all things necessary for His own glory, man's salvation, faith and life, is either expressly set down in Scripture, or by good and necessary consequence may be deduced from Scripture: unto which nothing at any time is to be added, whether by new revelations of the Spirit, or traditions of men. Nevertheless, we acknowledge the inward illumination of the Spirit of God to be necessary for the saving understanding of such things as are revealed in the Word: and that there are some circumstances concerning the worship of God, and government of the Church, common to human actions and societies, which are to be ordered by the light of nature, and Christian prudence, according to the general rules of the Word, which are always to be observed. (1.6)

This brief definition of sufficiency is superb in being both bold and circumspect. It makes the fact of sufficiency clear, and spells out its main consequences with regard to subsequent traditions and claimed revelations. It takes account of the fact that not every true doctrine can be read straightforwardly out of Scripture, but that some need to be deduced from it through the use of biblically shaped reasoning (a classic example being the doctrine of the Trinity). It also firmly warns off those who would imagine that Scripture intends to speak with decisive clarity on every issue on which it touches, and in this regard mentions explicitly the ordering of corporate worship, and church government.

Many scholars have argued that in the seventeenth and eighteenth centuries orthodox Protestant theology shifted significantly in its understanding of the roots of the authority of Scripture from the position of the first-generation Protestant Reformers, and that the Westminster Confession is typical of the new position. The argument runs like this: whereas the first Reformers consistently related Scripture to its role within God's purposes to redeem creation, their successors based the authority of Scripture on the fact of its having been inspired by God, and thereby removed Scripture somewhat from the central aspects of God's saving action in the world.

Two points can be made in response to this. First, since God inspired Scripture, according to 2 Timothy 3:16, precisely in order to teach about Christ and to train people in righteousness, it is not at all clear that linking the authority of Scripture to inspiration moves Scripture very far at all from the heart of God's saving purposes. Secondly, the above quotation from the Westminster Confession bases Scripture's authority primarily on its nature as God's Word, rather than directly on its inspiration (remembering, of course, that to understand Scripture as 'Word', in the sense given in the previous two chapters of this book, is integrally related to understanding it as 'breathed out' by God).[16]

The biblical and theological outlines of the previous two chapters now need to come into play, shaping how we ought to express the sufficiency of Scripture. Those chapters spoke of Scripture as 'the book of the covenant', and as the means by which God extends his action, and therefore himself, into the world in order to act communicatively in relation to us. In the light of this, I would define the sufficiency of Scripture in this way: *because of the ways in which God has chosen to relate himself to Scripture, Scripture is sufficient as the means by which God continues to present himself to us such that we can know him, repeating through Scripture the covenant promise he has brought to fulfilment in Jesus Christ.* Although I have just defended the post-Reformation theologians against the charge that their doctrine of Scripture departed significantly from that of the Reformers, I do intend this definition of sufficiency to relate Scripture directly to God's redemptive action more explicitly than some formulations of sufficiency from the seventeenth and eighteenth centuries do.

As with all doctrinal definitions, the one just offered is significant as much for what it does not state and what it does not do, as for what it does. It does not replace a living, dynamic relationship with the Lord with the study of a book. Instead it asserts that the

---

16. The most detailed description of post-Reformation orthodox Protestant theologians on this topic is in Richard Muller, *Post-Reformation Reformed Dogmatics*, who defends them against the charge that they largely abandoned the position held by the earlier Reformers.

Lord who wants to create living relationships with people comes
to establish those relationships through the Scriptures. Nor does it
put an obsession with the study of Scripture in the place the Holy
Spirit should occupy in the life of a believer, for it does not rule
out the need for the materially sufficient content of Scripture to be
brought into our minds and hearts, leading to saving trust in
Christ, through the illuminating work of the Spirit.

Nor does sufficiency decree that Scripture answers every question a believer might want to ask of it about matters relating to
church and life. Moreover the fact that Scripture touches on an
issue does not mean automatically that it speaks with great clarity
on that issue. There is much about church government, for
example, that many evangelicals hold dear, although often in disagreement with each other, that simply cannot be convincingly
demonstrated from Scripture either way.

Neither is it the case that belief in the sufficiency of Scripture
entails the view that biblical interpretation will be simple. Right
and healthy doctrine cannot always be read easily off the pages of
Scripture, but instead has to be worked for. The early church's
battles to define and defend the personhood of Christ as both
fully divine and fully human, and to outline the doctrine of the
Trinity, bear the clearest testimony to this. The Lord has given us a
Scripture in which his primary Word to us is clear, but that also has
depths with which we need to grapple.

The sufficiency of Scripture does not rule out the need for the
contemporary church to learn from, and give great weight to, the
church's traditions of belief and practice. I say more about the relation of Scripture to church and tradition in the next chapter.
However, for the time being we should note that each new generation of Christians does not come to Scripture with a clean slate.
Whether it acknowledges it or not, each generation approaches
Scripture wearing spectacles coloured by centuries of inherited
beliefs and practices. Where Scripture has faithfully shaped that
inheritance, Scripture proves itself sufficient again by being the
means through which God speaks again. Where that inheritance
includes purely human and thus unbiblical elements, the sufficiency
of Scripture stands as a call on us to open up all our most cherished
beliefs and practices, especially the ones we use to mark our

Christian subculture off from other subcultures, to correction by the voice of God in Scripture. For Scripture is sufficient as the means by which the Lord can lead us into greater covenant faithfulness.

The clarity of Scripture

The doctrine of the clarity of Scripture is particularly one that needs careful exposition,[17] because it has sometimes been stretched to claim more than can properly be said, both by those who are keen to make it central to their theology, and by those who wish to dismiss it. It was not, as we shall see, an innovation of the Reformation, although it did come into prominence as a consequence of the Reformation, and came to be applied to Christian life and thought with a new rigour.

The outstanding historical statement on the clarity of Scripture comes from Martin Luther, in his work *The Bondage of the Will* (Latin title *De servo arbitrio*), published in 1525. It was produced as a direct response to the *Diatribe or Conference concerning Free Will* (Latin title *De libero arbitrio diatribe sive collatio*), written a year earlier by the scholar Erasmus of Rotterdam.[18] The doctrine of the clarity of Scripture was at the heart of Luther's theological controversy with the Church of Rome. He argued against the idea that the teaching authority of the church has the final say in the interpretation of the Bible, and insisted instead that Scripture's ultimate interpreter is the Holy Spirit speaking through Scripture. This is what is meant by the short headline phrase 'Scripture is its own interpreter'. It is a claim that does not cut God out of the picture, but rather looks for his authoritative declaration of the meaning of his word to take place through the written word itself, not through appointed church teachers making supposedly decisive

---

17. The older term for this doctrine was the 'perspicuity' of Scripture, but that is often replaced by the (now clearer!) synonym 'clarity'.

18. For a helpful longer exposition of this debate, see Mark D. Thompson, *A Clear and Present Word: The Clarity of Scripture* (Leicester: Apollos; Downers Grove: IVP, 2006), pp. 143–150.

statements under the guidance of the Holy Spirit about the meaning of Scripture. Of course God uses teachers within the church to lead believers into the truth of the Bible. Yet these teachers are finite creatures and sinful people, and cannot be the ultimate means of God's authoritative pronouncement on the meaning of Scripture.

Erasmus had objected to the doctrine of the clarity of Scripture on the evidence of Scripture itself: that it speaks of a transcendent God, and that God within Scripture chooses to conceal many things. He also argued from the fact that there are so many disagreements about the right interpretation of Scripture that it cannot be clear in the way Luther had asserted.[19] In response Luther made an important distinction between what he called the 'internal' and 'external' clarity of Scripture. Many subsequent discussions of Scripture's clarity have fallen into obscurity by failing to observe this distinction. *Internal* clarity refers to what happens internally to the person reading or hearing the Bible when God the Holy Spirit opens their mind to understand it. It finds scriptural warrant in such texts as 1 Corinthians 2:14: 'The person without the Spirit does not accept the things that come from the Spirit of God but considers them foolishness, and cannot understand them because they are discerned only through the Spirit.' The *external* clarity of Scripture is the claim that the doctrine makes directly about Scripture itself: 'all that is in Scripture is through the Word brought forth into the clearest light and proclaimed to the whole world'.[20] In other words Erasmus was missing the point when he claimed that the multiplicity of interpretations, even among those who adhere to the doctrine of the clarity of Scripture, show that the doctrine is in error. Human finitude, and particularly sin, are the reasons for our lack of understanding of Scripture, rather than the cause being in some lack of clarity attributable to Scripture itself.

Luther is happy to acknowledge that some parts of Scripture remain obscure to us, but insists, 'If words are obscure in one place,

---

19. Ibid., pp. 144–145.

20. Martin Luther, *The Bondage of the Will*, tr. J. I. Packer and O. R. Johnston (Edinburgh: James Clarke, 1957), p. 74.

they are clear in another.' It is important to note that the basis of
this conviction is thoroughly theological and Christ-centred: 'what
solemn truth can the Scriptures still be concealing, now that the
seals are broken, the stone rolled away from the door of the tomb,
and that greatest of all mysteries brought to light – that Christ,
God's Son, became man, that God is Three in One, that Christ
suffered for us, and will reign for ever?' Christ is God's supreme revelation of his nature and purposes; Christ has not answered every
question that can be raised about God, but has revealed many things
with great clarity. The Bible, as the written word of God, must share
in that clarity, since our only access to God's revelation in Christ is
through the Scriptures, which speak of him, and through which he
also continues to speak. Therefore nothing of significance for the
gospel is contained in an obscure passage without being proclaimed
plainly elsewhere. To deny this is, for Luther, not just to engage in
theological debates about relatively insignificant topics, but is to
'Take Christ from the Scriptures'.[21] The doctrine is often defended
by reference to individual verses, such as Psalm 119:130:

> The unfolding of your words gives light;
>   it gives understanding to the simple.

However, individual verses like these give expression only to the
deeper biblical-theological bases of the doctrine Luther outlines.

As Luther recognized, it is the case that, while some things are
revealed, not everything is fully expounded for us in Scripture.
Thus Deuteronomy 29:29, 'The secret things belong to the LORD
our God, but the things revealed belong to us and to our children
for ever, that we may follow all the words of this law.' This remains
true even at later and fuller stages in the history of God's self-
revelation. The relations between the three persons of the Trinity,
and the union of divine and human natures in Christ, are examples
of theological issues not revealed in Scripture in a way that
answers every question we might ask about them. However, argues
Luther against Erasmus, this does not prove the obscurity of

---

21. Ibid., p. 71.

Scripture. Instead God has chosen to teach us plainly in Scripture *that* these things are so, but not *how* they are so. To claim that Scripture is clear is not to claim that it fully expounds every matter on which it touches, for God obviously determines that there are some things we do not need to know.[22] Such is the heart of Luther's impassioned response to Erasmus.

Anticipations of this full outworking of the doctrine of the clarity of Scripture can be found in the writings of the early church. Augustine famously asserted, 'almost nothing is dug out those obscure passages which may not be found set forth in the plainest language elsewhere'.[23] Similarly a second-century bishop of Lyons, Irenaeus, held that the principle by which Scripture should be interpreted is 'the canon of truth'. It may seem as if this puts Scripture under an interpretative principle separate from it, thereby implying its obscurity at significant points. However, this was not the case for Irenaeus, because he understood this 'canon' to be a summary of the message of Scripture, not a rule brought to bear on Scripture from elsewhere.[24]

Nevertheless through the first five centuries of the church the increasing tendency was to deny the clarity of Scripture. We noted previously that appeal was made in theological disputes to, as one writer famously put it, 'that which has been believed everywhere, always, and by all men'.[25] This is not an illegitimate move in itself, and was understandably adopted as a helpful strategy in countering those who argued in favour of heretical views, not by overtly criticizing Scripture but by reference to passages of Scripture. However, left unqualified, this kind of appeal to the authority of the church's universal (catholic) teaching to interpret Scripture was transformed over time into the establishment of the Roman ('Catholic') church as itself the appointed guardian and arbiter of the meaning of Scripture.

---

22. Ibid., p. 73.

23. Augustine, *On Christian Doctrine* 2.6.8.

24. See J. N. D. Kelly, *Early Christian Doctrines*, 5th ed. rev. (London: A. & C. Black, 1977), p. 39.

25. Vincent of Lérins, 'Commonitory', p. 38.

Looking to the period following the Reformation, it is often alleged that the doctrine of the clarity of Scripture underwent a significant (and unwelcome) development from the form in which Luther had expressed it. The charge is that there was a shift from an emphasis on the clarity of the *message* of Scripture to the view that, as one major proponent of this view has put it, clarity referred primarily to 'the words of Scripture, particularly in their semantic function'.[26]

This is an important issue to face, because in many areas of doctrine, such as adherence to the centrality of the clarity, sufficiency and authority of Scripture, contemporary evangelical thought is the direct descendant of orthodox Protestant doctrine in its post-Reformation form. If the notion of a shift in content between the Reformers and their successors in the following two centuries is basically correct, then the inherited form of the evangelical doctrine of Scripture can be portrayed persuasively as something of an aberration from authentic Reformation Protestantism. However, a careful reading of the main theologians suspected of introducing this change reveals that the accusation is unfairly made. For example, in the seventeenth century Francis Turretin speaks of the clarity of the 'sublime mysteries' revealed in Scripture. Similarly the Westminster Confession of Faith, written some thirty years before Turretin's great work, asserts that what is plain in Scripture is 'those things which are necessary to be known . . . for salvation' (1.7). The theological focus of the doctrine of the clarity of Scripture remained the semantic content of God's revelation.

Yet it is true there was an *additional* emphasis given by writers of the seventeenth and eighteenth centuries to the question of the very words of Scripture themselves. As one of the leading commentators on Reformed theology of the time has observed, it followed logically that at least the crucial biblical topics 'would have to be grammatically clear' if one part of Scripture can be said to shed light on other parts without appeal to the church as a decisive authority.[27] This is not just a point of general logic, but is also part of the logic of the theological character of Scripture in relation to

---

26. Berkouwer, *Holy Scripture*, pp. 272–275.

27. Muller, *Post-Reformation Reformed Dogmatics*, vol. 2, p. 341.

God, as the previous two chapters outlined it. It was argued there that Scripture is best conceived in overall terms as God's speech act, his covenant promise put into writing, such that to encounter Scripture is to encounter God in action. The verbal form of that divine action is a vital, and not an accidental, aspect of it; it is not a husk that can be discarded, revealing the supposed kernel. A covenant, or a promise, is what it is only by virtue of the words with which it is uttered. To say that the *message* is clear therefore is necessarily also to say something about the clarity of the *words*. If we suppose we can speak of the clarity of the message without also making assertions about the semantic clarity of the words, we are making the mistake of imagining that the language of Scripture functions in a way that goes against the grain of language as God has given it to us, and against the constant testimony of Scripture that to trust the words God has spoken is itself to trust God.

It was of course always possible that an additional doctrinal emphasis on the individual words of Scripture would come to eclipse the focus on the clarity of the message of Scripture those words serve to convey, and no doubt that occurred from time to time. However, it is important to realize the theological climate in which orthodox Protestant theologians of the seventeenth and eighteenth centuries were working. The attacks on their doctrines of Scripture became increasingly detailed and sophisticated during this period. They necessarily needed to defend their doctrines in similar detail, to avoid being accused of ducking the issues. It was unfortunate that, as often happens, their polemical arguments came to be treated as if they were the positive central points of their doctrines.[28] Nevertheless the most persuasive judgment on post-Reformation orthodox Protestant theology, including its doctrine of Scripture, remains that although the form in which theology was written changed significantly, being cast in a much more systematized form, the basic doctrinal content of the Reformation was retained.[29]

---

28. Richard Muller judges that this particularly happened in the second half of the seventeenth century (ibid., pp. 123–124).

29. See Martin I. Klauber, 'Continuity and Discontinuity in Post-

In the light of this historical review it is important to reflect on what the doctrine of the clarity of Scripture does *not* imply. This will help us, shortly, to articulate the heart of what it does imply.

10-13

Preaching and a clear Bible

The doctrine does not, first of all, imply that preaching is unnecessary. It is sometimes suggested that ironically the churches that most vociferously defend the clarity of Scripture are often also churches that put preaching at the very centre of their meetings. This emphasis on preaching, it is thought, is something of a denial of belief in Scripture's clarity. After all, if Scripture is so clear, why the need to explain it in public so often and at such length?

However, expository biblical preaching in fact assumes rather than denies the clarity of Scripture. An expository preacher takes it that his sermon can be judged as either a faithful or an unfaithful exposition of Scripture by his hearers, as they discern for themselves whether his teaching is or is not warranted by his biblical text. His appeal is not 'My teaching is true because I'm an officially appointed preacher,' nor is it at heart 'My teaching is true because I am a Spirit-filled and Spirit-anointed preacher.' Those two factors may give added weight to his teaching, but at heart the implied claim of the expository preacher is instead 'My teaching is true because it can be openly seen that what I am saying is in line with the meaning of Scripture.'

There is no doubt that the doctrine of the clarity of Scripture has often been brought into disrepute not so much because of theological qualms it raises, but because it has been invoked by certain church leaders and preachers to quash any questioning of views they are articulating: 'What I am saying is from the Bible, and the Bible is God's clear Word, so I must be right, and anyone who offers an alternative view from the Bible is by definition in error'; so runs the implied logic. Of course, though, the doctrine of the clarity of Scripture should lead to a rather different and humbler attitude in preachers and teachers. Since Scripture speaks with clarity to all, and since preachers are no less affected by sinful blindness towards divine teaching than any others, the right attitude for the preacher is constantly to be open to challenge and correction by others who read the same Scripture with illumination from the same Spirit as he does.

Moreover the doctrine of the clarity of Scripture does not claim that Scripture automatically has a power to explain itself whenever a part of it is read. A key function of good expository preaching is to explain the meaning and force of a passage when properly interpreted in the light of its different contexts: (1) the immediate literary context, (2) its context within the unfolding history of God's revelation, and (3) the context of the Bible as a whole. Such preaching, again, assumes that the doctrine of the clarity of Scripture applies primarily to Scripture as a whole, rather than to each individual paragraph. The preacher is not doing something with Scripture that the hearer *by definition* cannot do, which would be the case if the preacher were appealing primarily to special spiritual anointing or to his holding of an office in the church. He is doing something any Christian reader of Scripture could in principle do, if he or she had sufficient time and knowledge of Scripture.

Diverse interpretations and a clear Bible

We have already seen how Luther dealt with Erasmus' claim that the wide variety of interpretations of the Bible held by different people shows that the doctrine of the clarity of Scripture is untenable. Luther argued that the doctrine, strictly speaking, refers to Scripture as it conveys its message, rather than to the clear understanding of Scripture that occurs only by divine illumination. However, the fact of diverse interpretations of Scripture does raise questions that we have to face.

The initial observation must be that the *unanimity* of biblical interpretation through history is quite remarkable. On the fundamental questions of the character of God, the identity of Jesus Christ, and the nature of his saving action, Christians through history have been strikingly at one, despite divergences by some in different directions. It may be theoretically the case that, as critics allege, 'You can make the Bible say almost anything,' but the fact remains that strong unanimity on fundamental topics has been a feature of the history of the Christian church. However, what are we to make of disagreements between Christians who hold to the clarity of Scripture? An obvious solution is always to insist that Scripture is clear on the topic in question, but that the problem lies entirely with the frailty of human understanding. It is assumed that light will be shed on the topic in Scripture, through further prayer and study, so that unanimity will emerge.

This will indeed often be the case, but the doctrine of the clarity of Scripture does not imply that it is always the case. What, for example, do we make of evangelical disagreements over the baptism of infants born to believers? This is a classic example of a topic over which believers who share a high degree of doctrinal agreement have long been at odds with each other. The doctrine of the clarity of Scripture does not imply that in the Bible God always intends to teach clearly about every aspect of every topic on which the Bible touches. God commands his followers to make disciples and baptize them (Matt. 28:16–20), but strictly speaking Scripture contains no clear command on whether or not baptism is to be applied to the infants of believers. Some argue that the nature of the new covenant in Christ, as the fulfilment of God's overarching covenant with his people, means the infants of believers should be baptized. Others draw, from narrated biblical accounts of adults being baptized upon profession of faith in Christ, the conclusion that infants of believers should not be baptized. Some explicitly didactic texts refer to baptism, but the baptism of infants is not the main topic in view (e.g. Col. 2:12); another text mentions some spiritual benefit inherited by the children of a believing parent, but makes no explicit reference to baptism (1 Cor. 7:14).

It is tempting to assume that adherence to the doctrine of the clarity of Scripture must urge us on to seek unanimity, by both persuading others of our own interpretation and being open to correction by others. It is still theoretically possible, under God, that Christians with an evangelical doctrine of Scripture will one day find that such unanimity emerges on the question of infant baptism. However, such an expectation is not required by the doctrine of the clarity of Scripture. It is perfectly possible to affirm the doctrine in the form in which Luther did, and still say that God in Scripture does not intend to teach definitively about the appropriateness or otherwise of the baptism of the infants of believers. We extend the doctrine of scriptural clarity too far when we assume that there will be clear teaching in the Bible on every topic of which the Bible makes mention. When the doctrine has been overextended in this way, below the surface there has often been a model of Scripture at work that sees Scripture as primarily a compendium of divine teaching, out of which doctrine can be mined and pieced together in systematic fashion. This results in the desire to seek clear instruction on every topic mentioned in the Bible, because 'instruction' is the controlling model of the nature of Scripture. The model of Scripture proposed in this book, however, does not deny that Scripture contains a great deal of divine instruction, but offers a fundamentally richer model of Scripture, as God's communicative act in which he presents to us his covenant promise fulfilled in Christ. The heart of the doctrine of the clarity of Scripture refers to this act of God above all.

Defining the clarity of Scripture

This provides a helpful standpoint from which to consider two recent evangelical definitions of the clarity of Scripture, which I quote here (italics added):

> The clarity of the Scripture means that the Bible is written in such a way that its *teachings* are able to be understood by all who will read it seeking God's help and being willing to follow it. (Wayne Grudem)[30]

> The clarity of Scripture is that quality of the biblical text that, as God's communicative act, ensures its *meaning* is accessible to all who come to it in faith. (Mark Thompson)[31]

In general terms, both of these are perfectly fine restatements of the traditional doctrine. The latter, especially, is informed by the kind of understanding of the nature of Scripture outlined in this

30. Wayne Grudem, *Systematic Theology: An Introduction to Biblical Doctrine* (Leicester: IVP, 1994), p. 108.

31. Thompson, *Clear and Present Word*, pp. 169–170.

book. Yet they do differ from each other: Thompson's use of the
term 'meaning', following on from the reference to Scripture as
'God's communicative act', helps to keep the focus rightly on the
clarity of God's dynamic presence in and through the words of
Scripture. This contrasts with Grudem's more general and poten-
tially more wide-ranging term 'teaching'.

And they both differ in two ways from one classic definition
from the seventeenth century, from the pen of Francis Turretin.
He begins his discussion of the doctrine, setting it in his usual
question-and-answer format, thus: 'Are the Scriptures so perspicuous [clear] in things necessary to salvation that they can be
understood by believers without the external help of oral tradition
or ecclesiastical authority? We affirm against the papists.' And he
summarizes: 'The question then comes to this – whether the
Scriptures are so plain in things essential to salvation . . . that
without the external aid of tradition or the infallible judgment of
the church, they may be read and understood profitably by believers. The papists deny this; we affirm it.'[32]

First, in contrast to Grudem's definition, which speaks of the
clarity of Scripture's 'teaching', and to Thompson's, which refers to
its 'meaning', Turretin explicitly limits scriptural clarity to things
necessary and essential to salvation. A similar limitation is evident in
the statement on Scripture's clarity in the Westminster Confession
of Faith, which begins with a clear statement of what clarity does
not entail:

> All things in Scripture are not alike plain in themselves, nor alike clear
> unto all; yet those things which are necessary to be known, believed, and
> observed, for salvation, are so clearly propounded and opened in some
> place of Scripture or other, that not only the learned, but the unlearned,
> in a due use of the ordinary means, may attain unto a sufficient
> understanding of them. (1.7)

---

32. Francis Turretin, *Institutes of Elenctic Theology*, vol. 1, *First Through Tenth
    Topics*, tr. George Musgrave Giger, ed. James T. Dennison, Jr.
    (Phillipsburg: Presbyterian & Reformed, 1992), 2.17.1, 2.17.7.

Secondly, Turretin makes explicit the polemical aim of the doctrine. He is asserting that God speaks through Scripture about salvation in Christ in such a clear and self-authenticating way that the message does not have to be illuminated or validated by any individual or institution in order to be understood and accepted. The positive claim of the clarity of Scripture is given clear definition, and set within proper limits, when this polemical context is made plain. Without that context given in our definition of biblical clarity we risk giving the impression that individual believers, with no reference to preaching, teaching or good biblical scholarship, and therefore deprived of the traditions of biblical interpretation mediated through these channels, ought to be able to make good sense of Scripture on their own. The Spirit may graciously allow them to do that, but there is no promise from God that he unfailingly will. The doctrine should function primarily as a rejection of the notion that God speaks especially through a Spirit-filled individual, or through the teaching office of the church, to provide the meaning of his written word. Put in these terms, its ongoing relevance is plain.

Some individuals pick up a Bible, with no one to explain it to them, and find the gospel of Christ coming across loud and clear. Others, though, ask for God's help and read Scripture with an open spirit, but find that the gospel of Christ is not especially clear to them without a teacher to teach them the gospel from Scripture and to show them how to read Scripture (cf. Acts 8:30–35). These observations are evidence neither for nor against the clarity of Scripture, unless one starts with an overextended understanding of it. In this light, the definitions of both Grudem and Thompson risk suggesting a situation that is too individualized, supposing that the primary situation in view is that of someone reading the Bible on their own who finds the meaning of most of its paragraphs to be clear.

However, when we assert the doctrine of the clarity of Scripture we are asserting something at root both more general and more profound. Namely (and here is my own, admittedly longer, definition of scriptural clarity) we are asserting that

- Scripture is the written word of the living Word, God's
  communicative act, and the Spirit who authored it chooses
  to continue to speak most directly through it.

- Therefore we are right to trust that God in Scripture has spoken and continues to speak sufficiently clearly for us to base our saving knowledge of him and of ourselves, and our beliefs and our actions, on the content of Scripture alone, without ultimately validating our understanding of these things or our confidence in them by appeal to any individual or institution.[33]

This is intended as a contemporary restatement in the tradition of Turretin's formulation. It agrees with Turretin that the doctrine follows from the nature of Scripture as the book of the covenant: '[the Scriptures] are to us in place of a testament, contract of a covenant or edict of a king, which ought to be perspicuous and not obscure'.[34] It is this that Luther was getting at in his assertion that, because of Christ, there is nothing taught in an obscure part of Scripture that is not also taught in plain words elsewhere in Scripture.

The church can and sometimes must undergo revolution, and an individual can be called to repentance and faith, simply on the basis of God presenting himself clearly, as a God to be known and trusted, through the words of Scripture. That is the case whether or not the textual meaning is understood by people reading Scripture on their own, or being guided to see its meaning for themselves by a more knowledgeable teacher. This is the dynamic focus of the doctrine of the clarity of Scripture, and it flows from Scripture's integral relationship to the saving actions of God in Christ.

The authority of Scripture

The nature of biblical authority
The authority of the Bible is often the first claim evangelical believers want to make about the Bible. Of course for others it is the key

---

33. For a similar contemporary statement regarding the Reformers' view of Scripture, see Anthony C. Thiselton, *New Horizons in Hermeneutics* (London: HarperCollins, 1992), pp. 184–185.
34. Turretin, *Elenctic Theology* 2.17.11.

thing about the Bible that they wish to deny. In these long debates a crucial point is often overlooked. The phrase 'the authority of Scripture' must be understood to be shorthand for 'the authority of God as he speaks through Scripture'. To speak about the authority of Scripture is really to say more about God, and about the ways he chooses to act and speak in the world, than it is to say something directly about Scripture itself. The authority of Scripture is dependent entirely on the authority of God, and comes about only because of what God has chosen to do in the way he authored Scripture, and because of what he continues to do in presenting himself to us through Scripture as a God we can know and trust.

The authority of God, as the Bible describes his nature and his actions, is fundamental to his divine nature. Moreover, to speak of the authority of a book of any kind is really to make a claim about the authority of the book's author. For example, the British 'Highway Code' is authoritative over any other book that purports to explain the rules of the road because it is the government's own explanation of those rules. Or if one encyclopedia is said to be more authoritative than another, that is really a comment about its authors, asserting that they did better research and used more reliable sources in compiling their book than did the authors of other encyclopedias. Therefore to speak of the authority of Scripture is not at heart to say something about what Scripture is in itself. It is rather to make a claim about what Scripture is in relation to the unquestionably sovereign God, because what Scripture 'is' can only be properly defined in relation to God and his actions. The authority of Scripture is a statement about what God did in authoring Scripture, and about how he continues to act in relation to Scripture.[35]

---

35. Bavinck draws a close parallel between the character of the authority of God, and that of Scripture: 'The authority with which God acts in religion . . . is absolute, yet resistible. It invites and pleads yet is invincible. So also it is with the authority of Scripture . . . Before it, all else must yield . . . Its authority, being divine, is absolute . . . [but] It does not need the support of the church and does not conscript anyone's sword and inquisition. It does not desire to rule by coercion and violence but seeks free and willing recognition' (Bavinck, *Reformed Dogmatics*, vol. 1, p. 465).

It is precisely this subject that this book has focused on throughout. I offered an outline of the Bible's message of how God spoke out the words of the Bible, and how he chooses to continue to relate himself to them, as his ongoing communicative action in the world. Then I expressed this biblical material in a more systematic theological form, defining Scripture as the means by which the Father presents himself to us as the faithful God of the covenant, and by which the Son, the Word of God, speaks his words to us, and whose message and words the Holy Spirit himself spoke, oversaw and now illumines for us. All of this is what I am referring to and building on, when I talk about the authority of Scripture.

In addition the earlier sections of this chapter expounded this material in more doctrinal form. We have seen, in the light of the previous biblical and theological expositions, that Scripture is necessary. It is necessary because of the nature of the relationship God chooses to establish with us, as our trustworthy, promise-making and promise-keeping God. It is also necessary because of the relationship he requires from us towards him in return, which is one of trust, love and obedience. He could not present himself to us as such a God in anything other than verbal and written form, and we could not respond to him as we should without such a Scripture. We have seen, too, that it follows naturally that Scripture is sufficient as a means by which God presents himself to us, as a God to be known and trusted. And we saw that, since God has produced Scripture as the means by which he will act in this way, it is also the case that Scripture is sufficiently clear, as the basis on which we may know God and respond in covenant faithfulness to him.

To proclaim 'the authority of Scripture' does not add anything substantive to all this. It is, rather, one way in which we can usefully talk about the sum of all these parts. It is really a way of summarizing all that this book outlines. It states that we believe that all of this is true, that the sovereign God has indeed authored Scripture this way and chooses to relate to us in this way through Scripture. It commits us to giving the Bible the sovereign place in our lives that must follow from its central place in relation to God and his actions.

Inerrancy and infallibility

In what now follows I shall affirm and defend the inerrancy of Scripture. As I begin this discussion, it is important to be clear what I think I am doing in this section, and why I am addressing this topic in a subsection under the heading of the authority of Scripture. What I shall say here about the question of the inerrancy and infallibility of Scripture should not be thought of as the doctrinal climax to which the previous sections in this chapter have been leading. Nor should it even be thought of as a section to be set alongside Scripture's necessity, sufficiency, clarity, and consequent authority, equal in significance to those topics. Instead the claim that Scripture is inerrant is an outworking of the authority of Scripture. Specifically it is an outworking of the *trustworthiness* of Scripture, which I have been describing and defending throughout, and which follows from Scripture's identity as God's breathed-out word. And although I am discussing inerrancy under the heading of the authority of Scripture, it is not the key point to be made about Scripture's authority. I have already said what I think is most significant about the nature of biblical authority in the preceding paragraphs. Therefore, as well as making clear in this section what I think we ought to say about inerrancy, I want also to make clear why I do not think that the topic merits inclusion in its own right within a list of basic doctrinal assertions about Scripture. In other words I shall argue that inerrancy is a true statement to make about the Bible, but is not in the top rank of significant things to assert about the Bible.

Some British readers may be less familiar with debates about inerrancy, because they have often been at their fiercest in North America. It is important to start by defining the key terms, in order to be clear precisely which claims about the Bible we are considering here. As in many debates, confusion often arises when different groups attach different definitions to the primary terms. That has sometimes happened with the issue of 'infallibility and inerrancy', and we must avoid falling into that trap.

The idea that the Bible is 'infallible' means that it does not deceive. To say that the Bible is 'inerrant' is to make the additional claim that it does not assert any errors of fact: whether the Bible refers to events in the life of Christ, or to other details of history and geography, what it asserts is true.

Although inevitably there are several different variants of each viewpoint, a typical 'infallibilist' would argue that the Bible is entirely trustworthy in its aim of bringing us to salvation in Christ, and teaching us what the apostle Paul in the letter to Titus calls 'the truth that leads to godliness' (Titus 1:1). Therefore where the Bible makes claims about events in history that are intrinsically bound up with salvation and godliness, infallibilists would defend its historical reliability. Thus the biblical teachings that Christ died on a cross in a certain place outside Jerusalem, that he rose physically from the dead and was seen by certain groups of people, are historically accurate. However, an infallibilist would not worry too much about allegations that some of the Bible's more small-scale historical assertions are wrong. Infallibilism can grant that some of the details of time and place in the Gospels might be wrong, without concluding that the Bible's teaching on salvation and godliness is unreliable.

By contrast, a typical 'inerrantist' argues that every assertion that the Bible makes must be taken to be true, and this includes not just its statements about salvation and godliness, but also what it states about history and geography. A classic statement of this view is the 'Chicago Statement on Biblical Inerrancy', drawn up by a large group of evangelical scholars in 1978. Its twelfth article states, 'We affirm that Scripture in its entirety is inerrant, being free from all falsehood, fraud, or deceit. We deny that biblical infallibility or inerrancy are limited to spiritual, religious or redemptive themes, exclusive of assertions in the field of history and science.'[36]

It is important here to clarify three aspects of the mainstream inerrantist position. First, it is not the case, as is often stated, that commitment to biblical inerrancy is an invention of a Western rationalistic Christianity since the Enlightenment. It is sometimes said that the doctrine of inerrancy was first propounded by theologians of Princeton Seminary in the nineteenth century, as an aspect of their desire to present Christian theology as a scientifically credible discipline. It is indeed true that the term 'inerrancy' became

---

36. The whole statement is reproduced as Appendix 1 in J. I. Packer, *God Has Spoken* 2nd ed. (London: Hodder & Stoughton, 1993).

widely used only in the nineteenth century. It is also the case that through the eighteenth and nineteenth centuries the question of whether or not the Bible contains factual errors became a more significant one in arguments raised against Christian faith, and also therefore became much more prominent in theological thinking and writing that attempted to defend Christianity. However, the notion that Scripture was not widely believed to be entirely free of error before the nineteenth century has been carefully debunked. Thus the *term* 'inerrancy' may be of recent origin, but the *idea* of inerrancy is not. The historian Mark Noll states as his conclusion, 'the conviction that God communicates in Scripture a revelation of himself and of his deeds, and that this revelation is entirely truthful, has always been the common belief of most Catholics, most Protestants, most Orthodox, and even most of the sects of the fringe of Christianity'.[37]

Nor is it the case that inerrancy flows only out of a piece of faulty reasoning, wrongly imposing on God the idea that he must have produced an inerrant Scripture because he is a perfect God, and thereby in some way inappropriately limiting God's sovereign freedom to use an errant Scripture for his purposes if he so wishes. Some have argued that the doctrine of inerrancy makes the mistake of deciding in advance what God could and could not have done in the authoring of Scripture, and then drawing its conclusions about Scripture on that basis, rather than looking first with an open mind at what kind of Scripture God has in fact produced. It may well be that some supporters of inerrancy have sounded as if they were making just that mistake, but it is certainly not the case that this is the proper basis for the doctrine. Instead the claim that the Bible is inerrant is a conclusion drawn directly from what Scripture says about God, and about itself in relation to

---

37. Quoted in A. T. B. McGowan, *The Divine Spiration of Scripture: Challenging Evangelical Perspectives* (Nottingham: Apollos, 2007), p. 85. See also John D. Woodbridge, *Biblical Authority: A Critique of the Rogers/McKim Proposal* (Grand Rapids: Zondervan, 1982); and the essays by W. Robert Godfrey, John D. Woodbridge and Randall H. Balmer, in D. A. Carson and John D. Woodbridge (eds.), *Scripture and Truth* (Leicester: IVP, 1983).

God. Scripture says, as we have seen, that it is breathed out by God, as his own words. In addition, in Scripture God states with great clarity that his character is such that he cannot lie, and that he alone is utterly truthful and trustworthy (Titus 1:2; Heb. 6:18). The conclusion that the Bible is inerrant is essentially derived from linking these two related truths closely together. That is, it is a doctrine that can be shown to be a clear implication of what Scripture says about the character of God, and about the way his character shapes his action as the author of Scripture. God has chosen to tie Scripture to himself as his word in action, and therefore (as we saw in the biblical outline chapter) Scripture's speech acts are an aspect of God in action in the world. It is therefore right to conclude that Scripture's words will borrow their qualities from God.

A second clarification about inerrancy is important. Belief in biblical inerrancy naturally takes account of a number of features of Scripture that flow from the fact that it is written in ordinary human language, using the everyday features of ordinary language. These include the use of round numbers and colloquial approximations; loose and free quotations (especially of the Old Testament in the New); some unusual (and, strictly speaking, wrong) grammatical forms; and figures of speech such as metaphor, parable, hyperbole and so on.[38] None of these features counts against the claim that Scripture does not err in everything it affirms. Rather it is by taking full account of these features that we shall be able to discern what in fact God is and is not asserting in Scripture.

One straightforward example is the early chapters of Genesis. The question of how much of the content of these chapters is intended by God to give historical description and how much is intended to be metaphorical is of course widely debated among evangelicals. However, subscribing to inerrancy does not require us to adopt one particular interpretation of these chapters – for example, believing that the universe was created in six twenty-four hour periods. Many inerrantists believe that Genesis does intend to teach this, while many other inerrantists believe that it

---

38. See Grudem, *Systematic Theology*, pp. 91–92, for helpful examples of some of these features.

does not. Inerrancy does not set down any principle that requires certain sections of Scripture to be treated as intended to be either largely historical or largely metaphorical. That question must be addressed through appropriate biblical interpretation, and the answer is not determined in advance by a doctrine of Scripture. All inerrantists, however, do agree that whatever one decides that Scripture intends to assert, that content must be regarded as free from error.

A third and final clarification of inerrancy is in order. It is sometimes thought that belief in inerrancy flourishes only when Scripture is regarded as primarily a compilation of statements of fact about God, humanity and the world. I have argued at some length in the earlier sections of this book that Scripture is far more than that, not least because no human language ever has the primary function of just stating facts. Scripture of course states many facts, and asserts many propositions, but those assertions are always just an aspect of the more profound function of Scripture as the means by which God chooses to act in relation to us, making himself known to us as the faithful Lord of the covenant.

When a search is launched for those theologians or Christian groups who might have turned Scripture from a living Word into a compendium of facts, the usual suspects rounded up and brought in for questioning are the nineteenth-century and early twentieth-century theologians from Princeton Seminary, especially Warfield and Hodge. Indeed living as they did in an era in which scientific rationality loomed large as a criterion by which every claim to truth was to be tested, and affected as they inevitably were by the culture surrounding them, it is unsurprising that some of their statements and approaches to Scripture seem to be more interested in facts stated in Scripture than in God's dynamic action in and through Scripture.

These, then, are the two basic positions, infallibility and inerrancy, with three clarifications of what inerrancy does and does not entail. In ongoing debates on these issues, clearly some evangelicals are led to reject 'inerrancy' not so much because they disagree with what it claims about Scripture, but more so because they disagree with the central position some inerrantists give to the doctrine within their doctrine of Scripture.[39] However, misgivings about how some *use* the doctrine of inerrancy should not lead us to reject the doctrine *itself*. We could summarize it thus: inerrancy is no more and no less than a *natural implication* of the fact that Scripture is identified as the speech act of a God who cannot lie, and who has chosen to reveal himself to us in words.[40] Each half of this phrase warrants a little explanation.

First, *inerrancy is no more than a natural* implication *of inspiration*. It may be a true statement to make about Scripture; indeed as I have argued briefly, it is true. Yet, although it is true, we should not make too much of it theologically. Inerrancy is a claim about Scripture's *propositions*. The reason that inerrancy ought not to occupy a central place in our doctrine of Scripture is that, if it does, we are taking just one aspect of Scripture's content, its propositional statements, and building our doctrine of Scripture on it. The core of our doctrine of Scripture is then likely to down-play what is in fact the fundamental characteristic of Scripture,

---

39. One very recent example is A. T. B. McGowan, in his book *The Divine Spiration of Scripture*. Around half the book focuses on inerrancy. McGowan certainly states along the way that he does not believe that the original biblical manuscripts were free from error: '[God] did not give us an inerrant autographical text' (McGowan, *Divine Spiration*, p. 124). Yet by the end of his book it seems the main reason for his rejection of inerrancy is not so much that he is convinced the Bible really does contain errors; he may think it does, but that is not his main point. He says in conclusion, 'my rejection of the use of the term "inerrancy" does not mean that I am arguing for "errancy". I am simply saying that to speak of inerrant *autographa* is not the way to present and defend a "high" view of Scripture' (McGowan, *Divine Spiration*, p. 210). (The *autographa* are the original biblical documents, as written by the first authors, which have not survived.) In my view, McGowan is right in what he says about the *use* of the doctrine of inerrancy, but wrong to reject the doctrine *itself*.

40. Donald Macleod calls inerrancy a consequence of inspiration, not a quality of it (Donald Macleod, *A Faith to Live by: Understanding Christian Doctrine* [Fearn, Ross-shire: Mentor, 1998], p. 17).

which is the fact that through its words God performs acts of revelation and redemption. It will seem to others that we believe (and we ourselves may also come to believe) that the most important characteristic of Scripture is its propositional statements. It will then be hard not to have a distorted view of Scripture that treats it as primarily a collection of historical and theological propositions, rather than approaching it first of all as the means for God's revelatory and redemptive action towards us.

To say as one's primary claim for a text that it contains no errors may well be a true thing to say about it, but in the end it does not in itself say anything especially significant about it. (Presumably a good dictionary is error-free, but that does not raise its status above that of just a dictionary.) What is much more significant to say about a text is who wrote it, and what purposes the author intended to perform by means of it. We can happily assert inerrancy with conviction, while putting it in its right place in relation to other aspects of the doctrine of Scripture, and without it coming to occupy centre stage in our thinking about Scripture.

As a historical aside, I need to acknowledge that what I have just been arguing is somewhat controversial, and perhaps reflects the British context in which I write. J. I. Packer, whose writings on Scripture since the 1950s have made one of the most significant contributions to the maintenance and defence of the evangelical doctrine of Scripture, has said that in twentieth-century debates about Scripture it was especially in North America that

>
> biblical inerrancy was from the first made the touchstone more directly
> and explicitly than was ever the case in the parallel debates in Britain.
> This, I now think (I did not always think so), argues for clearer-
> sightedness in the New World, for without inerrancy the structure of
> biblical authority as evangelicals conceive it collapses.[41]

It may be the case that the key issue here is related to the point at which Scripture is being opposed in the circumstances in which we

---

41. J. I. Packer, *Truth and Power: The Place of the Bible in the Christian Life* (Guildford: Eagle, 1996), p. 91.

find ourselves. Indeed it is always important to distinguish doctrine from apologetics; doctrine unavoidably has an apologetic edge to it, but it is also true that Christian doctrine need not constantly reshape itself to address every passing accusation. Packer makes the case historically that, in the North American context in which he has long worked, the evangelical doctrine was undermined by some evangelicals themselves precisely at the point of biblical inerrancy, and so it needed to be defended most strongly at that point. That argues for inerrancy being brought to the fore when the situation calls for that move for apologetic reasons. My argument is more that, in constructing the doctrine of Scripture, we should stand back as much as possible from the heat of current battles (although of course we can never do so entirely) in order to think through our doctrine of Scripture biblically and theologically. When we do that, it emerges that inerrancy ought to be located systematically within our overall doctrine of Scripture in a less significant place than it has sometimes been given.

Inerrancy is thus no more than an *implication* of inspiration. *Yet neither is it anything less than a* natural *implication of inspiration.*[42] It is a true feature of Scripture, flowing from the character of God, and from the fact that he has chosen to relate to us through words he speaks to us. The speech acts in Scripture through which God speaks to us include many statements that claim to be statements of fact. As argued in an earlier chapter, language never exists simply to state propositions: its primary role is as a means by which one person acts in relation to others. To place a great deal of theological weight on inerrancy makes the mistake of treating language as if its primary purpose is to state propositions, when the stating of propositions is something language does as part of a much more profound action. However, to reject inerrancy in favour of infallibility is to make the mistake of pretending that the purposes for which God spoke Scripture can safely be separated

---

42. In this regard McGowan is wrong when he appears to imagine that, in order to avoid grounding scriptural authority on inerrancy, he needs to take the further step of trying to sit light to the question of whether or not Scripture contains errors.

/0 - 20

from many of the propositional statements he makes through Scripture, leaving us to trust his purposes in Scripture, while questioning many of his propositional statements. If we try to make this kind of separation, we do violence to the coherent nature of the speech acts of Scripture, and we make a distinction between Scripture's overall purpose and its individual statements that Scripture itself never makes. In addition, we fail to acknowledge the fact that a great deal of God's revelation of himself and of his purposes takes place in the details of the history Scripture narrates, and is inextricably bound up with those details.

The place I recommend should be assigned to inerrancy within the doctrine of Scripture accords well with Herman Bavinck's treatment of it. Nowhere does he devote a section specifically to the discussion of inerrancy; nor does he go out of his way to defend it in detail. It is perhaps this feature of his doctrine of Scripture that has led some to conclude that he does not really hold to inerrancy. Yet this is not a tenable position. Responding to those who would deny inerrancy, Bavinck rejects the view that 'the historiography of Scripture is untrue and unreliable'. While acknowledging the profound human character of Scripture, he likens it to the perfect humanity of Christ: 'just as Christ's human nature, however weak and lowly, remained free from sin, so also Scripture is "conceived without defect or stain"; totally human in all its parts but also divine in all its parts'.[43] Thus, while he regularly asserts the full truthfulness of Scripture, he does so along the way, constantly keeping in view God's deeper redemptive purpose in giving us Scripture.

One final question needs to be asked about inerrancy. If we subscribe to inerrancy, what should our approach be to apparent or alleged errors within Scripture? The answer to this question depends very much on the kind of error that has been alleged.

---

43. Bavinck, *Reformed Dogmatics*, vol. 1, pp. 447, 435. See further on this, Richard B. Gaffin, Jr., *God's Word in Servant-Form: Abraham Kuyper and Herman Bavinck on the Doctrine of Scripture* (Jackson, Miss.: Reformed Academic, 2008). I am grateful to David Gibson for bringing this book to my attention.

Two kinds deserve mention here. Some historical details in Scripture are called into question by the current state of archaeological research. In such cases it needs to be remembered that such scientific study is regularly producing new discoveries and coming to new conclusions. Therefore final judgment often needs to be suspended in expectation of new evidence coming to light. Many books have been written demonstrating how different areas of archaeological research over the years have supported rather than contradicted Old Testament narratives.

In other cases it is argued that contradictory accounts of the same event are given in different places in Scripture, which cannot both be right. A sensible approach to such examples is not to rush to try and harmonize the differing accounts too quickly, because to do so risks missing the richness of the truth that God is teaching by having breathed out the two accounts. One theological example is the census of the people of Israel taken by king David. Chronicles says that it was Satan who incited David to take the census (1 Chr. 21:1), whereas 2 Samuel 24:1 makes the Lord in his anger out to be the one who incited David. Many people have stumbled over what they take to be this kind of theological inconsistency within Scripture, and conclude that Scripture as a whole cannot be taken as a trustworthy theological basis for faith. However, these parallel but differing accounts serve to give different but not contradictory insights into complex spiritual realities. In this case 1 Chronicles and 2 Samuel each reflect a different aspect of the ultimately mysterious relationship between the action of the sovereign Lord, and the actions of Satan within that sovereignty. That relationship is narrated most clearly in the early chapters of Job, where Satan acts explicitly within limits set by God, but then disappears from the scene, and the actions he has performed come to be regarded in the rest of the book as actions for which God is responsible.

Other examples are historical in nature. Did Jesus heal blind Bartimaeus on his way into Jericho (Luke 18:35), or on his way out (Mark 10:46)? How do we map out exactly the chronology of the events around Jesus' death from the different accounts of the four Gospels? Bible commentaries and books on difficult passages in the Bible often give different ways in which examples such as these can be accounted for. It is important, though, to take full acknowledgment of the apparent difficulty, and to be forced by it to read the Scriptures again with renewed care and insight. When we do so, it often emerges that the alleged error is only an apparent one. Thus it can cease to be an error when we realize that the Gospels do not claim to be offering an exhaustive account of Jesus' life, or to be relating verbatim everything he said on each occasion, or to be presenting all their material in exact chronological order. The church's understanding of the nature of the Gospels God has given us, and thus our ability to hear more clearly what he in fact says to us through them, has usually grown when Christians have reacted to allegations of error in Scripture not by seeking too quickly to explain the issue away, but by seeing themselves as sent back again to Scripture, to submit what we think it says still further to what it in fact does say.

5. THE BIBLE AND CHRISTIAN LIFE: THE DOCTRINE OF SCRIPTURE APPLIED

In this final chapter I turn to think through some of the primary ways in which the doctrine of Scripture ought to be applied to Christian thought and practice. The first section looks more closely at the question of *sola scriptura*, and builds explicitly on the doctrinal topics of the previous chapter. Subsequent sections look practically at the place and function of Scripture in the life of the church and of individual believers.

The meaning of *sola scriptura*

Sola scriptura is a Latin phrase meaning 'Scripture alone'. As we have seen, it emerged as one of the key phrases used to summarize the main theological points made by the Protestant Reformers of the sixteenth century. Indeed for many people *sola scriptura* still stands as a summary of what evangelical Protestantism is really all about, and especially of what is at stake in the evangelical doctrine of Scripture. Many contemporary evangelicals find themselves rallying most strongly towards slogans that proclaim 'Scripture alone'.

It is often the case in the history of the church that a doctrine is explained with clarity and conviction in one period, and then is slowly transformed over time into something rather different, but with its descriptive label still attached. That is especially so with *sola scriptura*. When it is described both by contemporary supporters and contemporary opponents, the doctrine in view often differs significantly from what we find in the writings of Luther, Calvin and other Protestant writers of past centuries. In other words many people who attack *sola scriptura* as unbiblical or illogical are attacking something different from the beliefs of the mainstream Reformers. Moreover, as we shall shortly see, many modern evangelicals who think of themselves as faithfully maintaining the legacy of Luther and Calvin have in fact drifted into a position those two great Reformers regularly condemned. In order to see our way clearly through this at times confusing situation, it is best to start early on in the history of Christian thinking on this topic.

The issue underlying *sola scriptura* is the question of the relationship between Scripture on the one hand and tradition, understood as some mixture of traditions of Christian thought, belief and practice, on the other. One theologian from the early centuries of the Christian church, Tertullian, regularly referred to something he called 'the Rule of Faith'. He says that our seeking after knowledge must always remain within the Rule. If we stray outside the boundaries set by the Rule, then we shall fall into error and heresy. The Rule was thus the interpretative context in which Tertullian argued that the Bible should be interpreted. It was made up of a summary of what Tertullian took to be the primary teachings of Scripture, and was shaped in the form of a confession of faith in the triune divinity of Father, Son and Holy Spirit.[1] The Rule is thus similar in form and content to what later became known as the Apostles' Creed.

When modern-day evangelicals encounter this teaching from Tertullian, some may want to ask why we need this Rule at all. Why

---

1. See Tertullian, *The Prescription against Heretics*, Ante-Nicene Fathers, vol. 3, ed. Alexander Roberts and James Donaldson (Peabody: Hendrickson, 1994), chs. 12–13.

not simply be content with Scripture? Why add some extraneous non-biblical 'rule' to it, and thereby seemingly undermine the sufficiency of Scripture? Tertullian's response to a question like this (as far as one can tell!) would likely be to explain that the questioner has misunderstood what he is doing. He was not at all *adding* something to Scripture, but rather providing a necessary tool to ensure that the fundamental teaching of Scripture was constantly upheld in the ongoing task of interpreting the Bible. For Tertullian was faced (as have been many subsequent generations of Christians) with people who claimed to be taking their beliefs from 'Scripture alone', but whose beliefs strayed far from orthodox Christian teaching. (Jehovah's Witnesses are a prime contemporary example.) How can such people be shown to be in the wrong? A central strategy used by Tertullian, and by many others in the early centuries of the church, was to assert the Rule of Faith as a summary of teaching already agreed to be a true summary of the message of the Bible. The Rule did not strike at the root of the sufficiency of Scripture; it was presented in order to uphold the ultimate authority of Scripture. To depart from the Rule was to depart from Scripture.

The Rule of Faith of course comes under the heading of what is often referred to as 'tradition'. For those brought up, as many contemporary Protestants have been, in the continuing aftermath of Reformation debates, which are normally described as pitching Scripture and tradition *against* each other, it needs to be pointed out very clearly that the early fathers of the church would simply not have understood the notion of Scripture clashing with tradition. One historian has said that Tertullian's Rule of Faith, similar to the conception of the 'canon of truth' outlined by Irenaeus, another early theologian, was not 'a formal creed, but rather the intrinsic shape and pattern of the revelation itself'.[2] Another writer on these early church fathers says it this way: 'The idea of the rule of faith as supplementing or complementing, or indeed adding anything whatever to the Bible, is wholly absent from their

---

2. J. N. D. Kelly, *Early Christian Doctrines*, 5th ed. rev. (London: A. & C. Black, 1977), p. 40.

thoughts; indeed such an idea would be in complete contradiction to their conception of the relation of the rule to the Bible.'[3] Thus at a very early stage in the life of the church, apostolic tradition and Scripture flowed together into the single stream of Scripture. The independence of tradition alongside Scripture disappeared, and the only way to assess a teaching as apostolic or not was by appeal to the apostolic writings that made up Scripture.[4]

In order to help us think clearly about the different ways in which Scripture and tradition can be related to one another, I shall use terms found in the writings of the twentieth-century historian Heiko Oberman.[5] These terms are helpfully clear, and have been adopted by a number of different writers on this topic. Oberman calls the predominant view held by the early church, and which we have seen in the writings of Tertullian, 'Tradition I'. It is the view that tradition is a tool to aid in the faithful interpretation of Scripture, expounding the primary teachings of Scripture, with Scripture remaining the only source of infallible divine revelation, to which the tradition is always subject.

Of course, although Tradition I was the predominant view of the church in the first five centuries, the picture was more varied than just being a succession of thinkers who copied Tertullian exactly. In the fourth century Basil of Caesarea seemed to take a significant step beyond Tertullian and Irenaeus when he referred to traditions outside Scripture believed to have been handed down from the apostles, which, he asserted, had the same force as Scripture.[6] Similarly, when Augustine explains how to reach clarity in biblical

---

3. R. P. C. Hanson, *Tradition in the Early Church* (London: SCM, 1962), p. 126.

4. This way of expressing it is drawn from Herman Bavinck, *Reformed Dogmatics*, vol. 1, *Prolegomena*, gen. ed. John Bolt, tr. John Vriend (Grand Rapids: Baker Academic, 2003), p. 485.

5. Heiko Augustinus Oberman, *The Harvest of Medieval Theology: Gabriel Biel and Late Medieval Nominalism*, rev. ed. (Grand Rapids: Eerdmans, 1967).

6. Basil of Caesarea, *Concerning the Holy Spirit* 66, Nicene and Post-Nicene Fathers, vol. 8, ed. Philip Schaff and Henry Wace (Grand Rapids: Eerdmans, n. d.).

interpretation, he urges that the Rule of Faith be consulted, which he says is to be gathered from Scripture's plainer passages *and from the authority of the church.*[7] When discussing the sufficiency of Scripture, we noted that in fact Augustine elsewhere makes unambiguous assertions of Scripture's material sufficiency. It is therefore unlikely that he intended by this statement to establish Scripture and church as two separate sources of authority. Rather he sees the church not as adding to the clear message of Scripture, but as reinforcing and teaching it. Indeed it has been debated whether or not Basil, in his statements on tradition, saw himself as actually establishing the church as an authority separate from Scripture.

However, whatever the intentions of Augustine and Basil, their statements sowed seeds that slowly germinated over the following thousand years. It was particularly during the period 1100–1400 that a different view of the relationship between Scripture and tradition developed, which regularly appealed back to these statements by Augustine and Basil. This view is called by Oberman 'Tradition II'. It asserts that there are two distinct sources of divine revelation, *Scripture* and *church tradition,* with the latter being handed down either orally or through customary church practices. Tradition II thus represents an outright denial of the sufficiency and clarity of Scripture, and of the unique authority of the Bible. A vital point to note is that this Tradition II was an innovation in Christian thought. It is doubtful that it was held with clarity by any of the church fathers, and it came to be developed only fairly late on in the Middle Ages. By the dawn of the Reformation, though, at the beginning of the sixteenth century, it had come to be the primary view held by the Roman ecclesiastical authorities, with whom the Reformers would find themselves in conflict. It remained true, however, that even in the late Middle Ages Tradition I was championed by many within the church, notable examples being John Wyclif and John Hus.[8]

---

7. Augustine, *On Christian Doctrine*, Nicene and Post-Nicene Fathers, vol. 2, ed. Philip Schaff (Grand Rapids: Eerdmans, 1956), 3.2.2.

8. See Keith A. Mathison, *The Shape of Sola Scriptura* (Moscow, Idaho: Canon, 2001), pp. 79–80.

Within this historical context, the Reformers saw themselves not as introducing some new teaching about 'Scripture alone', but as overturning the dangerous innovation brought in by the growth of Tradition II, and recovering for the church as a whole the early church's 'Tradition I' position. For the Reformers, *sola scriptura* meant a return to Tradition I. In other words the Reformers had a high regard for the authority of inherited traditions of biblical interpretation, and of the views of earlier generations of widely respected theologians, as well as for the church's role in providing a context in which Scripture can properly be understood.

This is especially evident in the ways they responded to an objection made to them. Augustine had once written, 'For my part, I should not believe the gospel except as moved by the authority of the catholic church.' The Catholic opponents of the Reformers liked to quote this to them, arguing that it demonstrated that the Reformers' understanding of the supreme authority of Scripture, needing no authorization from the church, was at odds with the greatest of the church fathers. None of the Reformers was content to respond that Augustine was simply wrong and that they were satisfied that they had been sufficiently anointed by the Spirit to have now discovered the truth. Instead they worked hard to demonstrate that Augustine was saying something with which they themselves agreed. As Calvin puts it, 'He meant only to indicate what we also confess as true: those who have not yet been illu-mined by the Spirit of God are rendered teachable by reverence for the church, so that they may persevere in learning faith in Christ from the gospel.'[9] A century later the Westminster Confession of Faith acknowledged the same point: 'We may be moved and induced by the testimony of the Church to an high and reverent esteem of the Holy Scripture . . .' (1.5).

One recent writer, Keith Mathison, has helpfully examined the doctrine of *sola scriptura* at some length. He summarizes the Reformers' doctrine with this frequently used phrase: 'our final

---

9. John Calvin, *Institutes of the Christian Religion*, Library of Christian Classics, vols. 20–21, ed. John T. McNeill, tr. Ford Lewis Battles (Philadelphia: Westminster, 1960), 1.7.3.

authority is Scripture alone, but not a Scripture that is alone'. Scripture is the only source of *revelation* needed for Christian faith and life, but it is not the only *thing* needed for Christian faith and life.[10] We need the Rule of Faith, as well as the historic creeds of the church, which are a fuller form of the Rule. We need the traditions and practices of the church's interpretation of Scripture in order to help us to walk faithfully in our understanding of and obedience to Scripture. The Reformers' conviction of *sola scriptura* is the conviction that Scripture is the only *infallible* authority, the only supreme authority. Yet it is not the *only* authority, for the creeds and the church's teaching function as important subordinate authorities, under the authority of Scripture.

In response to the Protestant Reformers the Roman Catholic Church hardened its 'Tradition II' position. In 1546 the Council of Trent decreed that 'saving truth and rules of conduct' are 'contained in the written books [of Scripture] and in the unwritten traditions'. Some contemporary Roman Catholics have argued that this does not express the idea that revelation comes in two separate sources, but rather that the same content comes to us in two different ways.[11] This argument has been accepted by some and rejected by others.[12] Yet it is certainly the case that, in the centuries following the Reformation, Roman Catholic teaching became entrenched in Tradition II.

Something else needs to be said about the context in which the Reformers developed their doctrine of *sola scriptura*. They were not responding just to the Roman Catholic 'Tradition II' position. On the other side were the divergent groups of believers normally now categorized as 'the Radical Reformation', or Anabaptists.[13]

---

10. Mathison, *Shape of Sola Scriptura*, pp. 257–259.

11. Josef Rupert Geiselmann, *Die Heilige Schrift und die Tradition* (Freiburg: Herder, 1962), p. 270.

12. Accepted by George H. Tavard, *Holy Writ or Holy Church: The Crisis of the Protestant Reformation* (London: Burns & Oates, 1959), pp. 242–245; rejected by Oberman, *Harvest of Medieval Theology*, p. 407.

13. For very brief portraits of several Anabaptist leaders, see Mathison, *Shape of Sola Scriptura*, pp. 124–125.

Diverse though these groups were, what they often had in common was a suspicious attitude to any inherited traditions of theology and practice. They discerned, along with the other Reformers, the serious errors of faith and practice into which the church had fallen. However, whereas the Reformers sought the solution to this in a return to the Tradition I position of the early church, the Radicals tried to flee from inheritance, and to derive their belief and teaching from 'the Bible alone'. Thus the Anabaptists' version of *sola scriptura* was very different from that of the other Reformers. It has recently been described (developing Oberman's terminology) as 'Tradition 0'.[14] It exalts the individual's interpretation of Scripture over that of the corporate interpretation of past generations of Christians. Within a Christian community it often comes to place great store on the interpretations of Scripture offered by an individual who claims to be, and is treated by others as a particularly Spirit-filled teacher, with little regard paid to the question of whether those teachings are significantly in line with the predominant teachings of the church throughout history.

Keith Mathison argues that this Tradition 0 position is so far removed from the Reformers' *sola scriptura* that it ought to be given a different label; he calls it 'solo *scriptura*'. He argues persuasively that since the eighteenth century American evangelicalism, particularly in its popular forms, has largely adopted something close to Tradition 0, while often wrongly imagining that it was remaining faithful to Luther and Calvin. It is certainly true that British evangelicalism has not been immune from the same malaise. One notable exception Mathison gives to this is the theology represented by Charles Hodge at Princeton Seminary in the nineteenth century.[15] He suggests that this mostly unintentional drift into the Anabaptist 'Tradition 0' was fuelled in America by two underlying factors: (1) Enlightenment philosophy, which stressed the individual as the arbiter of truth, distinct from traditions of thought, and

---

14. Mathison, *Shape of Sola Scriptura*, building on Alister McGrath's study of the Reformation.

15. Mathison, *Shape of Sola Scriptura*, pp. 142–149.

(2) a strong belief in the democratic rights of the individual.[16] In Europe the second of these factors may not have been as strongly politicized as across the Atlantic, but the first was certainly as influential.

There are many problems with 'Tradition 0'. The primary ones can be outlined here. It is clearly an innovation introduced into Christianity on a large scale only in the sixteenth century. Its most significant practical result has been the scandal of Protestant sectarianism, resulting in the multiplication of innumerable different Protestant denominations. One of Roman Catholicism's most powerful arguments against Protestantism is undeniably the proliferation of Protestant denominations over increasingly small issues of doctrine and practice, taking place with apparent disregard for the visible unity of the church. Now although it is often alleged that *sola scriptura* lies at the heart of the reasons for this sectarianism, *sola scriptura* in the Reformers' sense of that term (i.e. Tradition I) is not at fault here. Indeed they largely saw themselves as wanting to reform the church from within, rather than abandon it. The doctrine that has provided the impetus for the constant and easy splitting of one denomination and one church from another is not *sola scriptura*, but solo *scriptura*.

Moreover, as several critics point out, solo *scriptura* cannot account on its own terms for the collection of writings that form the canon of Scripture as we have it. The Bible does not come to us fully formed with the contents page breathed out by God. Instead the canon of Scripture was compiled over time – not by authoritarian decrees from church officials, but by gradual recognition across the churches of which books were inspired by God and which were not. Therefore the very contents page of the Bible is an inherited church tradition, widely recognized to be the correct one by the early generations of believers. In other words although it is certainly easy to *say* that one is doing without tradition, it is not actually possible to do without it.

---

16. Ibid., p. 239.

Even more widely than this, Herman Bavinck argues that tradition is necessary in order to link us back to Scripture as a whole. Scripture is certainly 'the living voice of God', but, since the times in which it was written,

> people, their life, thought, and feelings, have changed. Therefore a tradition is needed that preserves the connectedness between Scripture and the religious life of our time. Tradition in its proper sense is the interpretation and application of the eternal truth in the vernacular and life of the present generation. Scripture without such a tradition is impossible.[17]

This points out the necessary role of traditions of biblical interpretation for every new generation of Christian readers of the Bible, and very clearly defines what 'tradition' is in its positive sense. It also leads us to identify a further difficulty for Tradition o. Everyone who reads the Bible does so with a set of expectations and assumptions, some consciously held and some subconscious, that have been handed on to them. It is dangerous, of course, if these are misleading expectations and assumptions. What is often equally dangerous is to deny that one has them at all. Indeed, in practice, communities that espouse Tradition o cannot usually avoid adhering to some kind of tradition, in order to provide coherence in faith across the community, and to avoid falling into an anarchy in which each one does and believes simply what is right in his own eyes. They therefore smuggle 'tradition' in, without identifying it as such, in the form of the senior position in the community given to one or more individuals judged to be especially gifted in discerning the voice of the Spirit in Scripture. Some Tradition o communities, it is true, have managed to persist in exalting a very individualistic democratic approach to Scripture, in which every individual is allowed to be in effect 'his own pope'. But in practice most such communities have found it necessary to find cohesion around one 'anointed' individual, whose teachings establish contemporary 'traditions', while all the time arguing that

---

17. Bavinck, *Reformed Dogmatics*, vol. 1, p. 493.

all that is happening is that 'we are listening to God speak through the Bible'.

Thus *sola scriptura*, in its proper formulation as found in the thinking of the mainstream Protestant Reformers, is not what many of its modern critics or defenders imagine it is. It does not deny the necessity of traditions of biblical interpretation, credal formulations of biblical faith, and inherited church practices that help to express and pass on that faith. Rather it ensures that all those traditions serve Scripture, the supreme authority, rather than compete with it. *Sola scriptura* means 'Scripture supreme'.

Scripture and the Christian community

In this section we can continue to apply to the life of the church what has just been said about *sola scriptura*. The first task will be to enquire further into the relation of the subordinate authority of the church to the supreme authority of Scripture.

1 Timothy 3:15 calls the church 'the pillar and foundation of the truth'. This text provided Roman Catholic opponents of the Protestant Reformation with a basis for arguing that the authority of Scripture in fact rests on the authority of the church. Thus one Cardinal Perronius argued that Scripture's perfection and sufficiency are 'mediate', not 'immediate'. In other words Scripture sends us to the church, which supplements what Scripture lacks.[18] In response, Protestants turned to texts such as Ephesians 2:20, which speaks of the church as 'built on the foundation of the apostles and prophets, with Christ Jesus himself as the chief cornerstone'. This verse puts the church squarely on the foundation of the prophetic and apostolic writings, not vice versa. But, we might ask, how can this be fitted together with the church as 'the pillar and foundation of the

---

18. Quoted in Richard A. Muller, *Post-Reformation Reformed Dogmatics*, vol. 2, *Holy Scripture: The Cognitive Foundation of Theology* (Grand Rapids: Baker, 1993), p. 334.

truth'?[19] Francis Turretin explains that the church's function in relation to Scripture has five aspects.[20] It is the

- *keeper and preserver* of Scripture;
- *guide* that points people to Scripture;
- *defender* of Scripture, vindicating the genuine canonical books from the spurious ones;
- *herald* who proclaims the truth of Scripture;
- *interpreter* given the task of unfolding the true sense of Scripture.

'But all these', concludes Turretin, 'imply a ministerial only and not a magisterial power.'

As is typical of seventeenth-century orthodox Protestant theology, Turretin also explains in more philosophical terms what he means by the church having 'ministerial' authority, but not 'magisterial' authority:

> if the question is why, or on account of what, do I believe the Bible to be divine, I will answer that I do so on account of the Scripture itself which by its marks proves itself to be such. If it is asked whence or from what I believe, I will answer from the Holy Spirit, who produces that

---

19. It is perhaps noteworthy that the word sometimes translated 'foundation' in 1 Tim. 3:15 is not the more common New Testament word for 'foundation' (*themelios*), but is instead a word that appears only once in the New Testament (*hedraiōma*). Its precise meaning is unclear. It may refer to a building's foundations, but it may also refer to a building's 'mainstay' or 'buttress', which is how both Turretin and the recent English Standard Version of the Bible translate it. See George W. Knight III, *The Pastoral Epistles*, New International Greek Testament Commentary (Grand Rapids: Eerdmans; Carlisle: Paternoster, 1992), p. 181.

20. All the following references to Turretin are from Francis Turretin, *Institutes of Elenctic Theology*, vol. 1, *First Through Tenth Topics*, tr. George Musgrave Giger, ed. James T. Dennison, Jr. (Phillipsburg: Presbyterian & Reformed, 1992), 2.16.1–26.

belief in me. Finally, if I am asked by what means or instrument I believe it, I will answer through the church which God uses in delivering the Scriptures to me.

By way of illustration, Turretin observes that the authority of a human law rests not on the judges who uphold it and enforce it, but on the ruler who pronounces it. Thus the authority of Scripture rests ultimately only with the God who authored it and now speaks through it. However, human judges do function as the 'pillar and foundation' of the law, in that they guard, communicate and act upon it. Thus when the church expounds such doctrines as the Trinity, not found explicitly in Scripture, it is not making up for some insufficiency in Scripture by acting on an authority different from that of Scripture. Rather it is acting as a minister, drawing out truths implicit within Scripture itself.

Two further points can be seen to flow from this explanation of the relation of the church to Scripture. The first is that a strong doctrine of *sola scriptura* can fit perfectly well with a high view of the authority of the visible church. This needs pointing out quite forcefully in many modern evangelical circles, where it is often taken for granted that a high view of the authority of Scripture inevitably puts the right of individual believers to make their own judgments about the meaning of Scripture above that of the corporate judgment of the historical body of believers. For example, Article 20 of the Church of England's Thirty-Nine Articles, 'Of the Authority of the Church', states:

> The Church hath power to decree Rites or Ceremonies, and authority in Controversies of Faith; and yet it is not lawful for the Church to ordain any thing that is contrary to God's word written, neither may it so expound one place of Scripture that it be repugnant to another. Wherefore, although the Church be a witness and keeper of Holy Writ, yet as it ought not to decree any thing against the same, so besides the same ought it not to enforce any thing to be believed for necessity of Salvation.

This tightly packed statement clearly affirms the Reformers' understanding of both *sola scriptura* and the sufficiency of

Scripture, putting the church's application of Scripture clearly under the authority of what Scripture itself says. Yet it also gives to the church the authority to establish patterns of corporate worship that must be observed, as long as they cannot be shown to be contrary to Scripture. Indeed Article 34 of the Thirty-Nine Articles requires that anyone who openly breaks such patterns 'through his private judgment, willingly and purposely' should be openly rebuked, for offending against 'the common order of the Church . . . the authority of the Magistrate, . . . and the consciences of the weak brethren'. The point being made here is not that it is necessarily right to give such authority in these issues of corporate worship to a denominational or national church structure; that topic is not our concern here. Rather the point is that previous generations of Christians who believed thoroughly in the sufficiency of Scripture and *sola scriptura* also thought it quite consistent with those doctrines to give authority to the church in areas on which Scripture does not speak explicitly, and in matters on which faithful biblical believers found themselves in disagreement. If modern evangelicals often do not find themselves naturally fitting this kind of churchly authority together with *sola scriptura*, that would count as further evidence that the current common evangelical understanding is more akin to the 'solo *scriptura*' position described in the previous section than it is to the *sola scriptura* of the Reformers.

This contemporary evangelical suspicion about the authority of the church applies not only to evangelicals in hierarchical denominations. It is also often true of evangelicals whose view of the church excludes the exercise of authority over the local congregation from outside it. Mark Dever, the leader of a Baptist church in the United States, has recently bemoaned the lack of solid and loving application of church discipline in American churches.[21] There will be many identifiable reasons for the decline in the practice of church discipline in the twentieth century, but one must surely be the fact that the rise of 'solo *scriptura*' has made the exer-

---

21. Mark Dever, *Nine Marks of a Healthy Church*, rev. ed. (Wheaton: Crossway, 2004), pp. 167–193.

cise of any power by officers of the church over the individual believer seem untenable, for the individual has the Bible in his hand and claims to have the Spirit in his heart, just as firmly as do any of the leaders of his congregation. However, if we are clear on what is really meant by *sola scriptura*, then it is perfectly possible to fit alongside it a strong practice of church discipline and a robust view of the authority of the elders of the church.

The second application that flows from *sola scriptura* in relation to the church is that we need not, and indeed must not, deny the necessity of the church in enabling us to come to Scripture in the first place, and in helping us to be able to understand Scripture in the right way. On this topic the American theologian Stanley Hauerwas has written provocatively (thinking of churches in the United States) that *sola scriptura* 'is a heresy rather than a help in the Church'. He knows that the contemporary application of *sola scriptura* is often not what the Reformers intended. Indeed he judges that it has come to share much in common, surprisingly, with liberal biblical scholarship. Both, he says, 'share the assumption that the text of the Bible should make rational sense (to anyone) apart from the uses that the Church has for Scripture'. They both 'wish to make Christianity available to the person of common sense without moral transformation'.[22]

In fact Hauerwas subsequently goes too far in apparently arguing that the Scriptures have meaning only in so far as the church finds and lives out meaning in them.[23] Yet his main point is a helpful one. There are, it is true, some individuals who have read the Bible entirely on their own, without any encounter with communities of Christians, and who have found its message of redemption from sin through Christ's atoning work compellingly clear. They have put saving trust in Christ entirely on the basis of this solitary reading. However, such cases are rare, and seem to be special works of God's grace.

---

22. Stanley Hauerwas, *Unleashing the Scriptures: Freeing the Bible from Captivity to America* (Nashville: Abingdon, 1980), pp. 18, 27, 36,

23. See Timothy Ward, *Word and Supplement: Speech Acts, Biblical Texts, and the Sufficiency of Scripture* (Oxford: Oxford University Press, 2002), pp. 187–190.

The much more common pattern is that someone encounters a community of Christians, and learns how to approach Scripture, and how to open their mind and the eyes of their heart to its meaning and message, by taking on both some of the Christian community's ways of living, and its ways of reading the Bible. For myself, in evangelistic ministry in my own church, I rarely find that someone reaches an understanding of sin, the cross and grace without already having spent time with other Christians, observing how they read the Bible, and finding themselves already beginning to adopt, sometimes to their surprise, some godly behaviours and attitudes. It is not just that these people are noticing the transformed lives of believers, and so find the gospel more attractive. That is certainly happening, but additionally what is going on is that, as they begin to adopt some Christian habits and behaviour, they find the Bible's message coming through to them all the more clearly and compellingly. Faith in the God of the covenant is more comprehensible, and easier to take on for oneself, the more one aligns oneself with the attitudes and practices of the covenant community.

This is sometimes expressed by saying that 'belonging' usually must accompany or precede 'believing'. What we make of the evangelistic theory behind this kind of phrase is not something that concerns me here. My point is that it is perfectly consistent both to believe that it is very hard for most people to hear and respond to the gospel without in some way coming to belong to the community of believers and to take on at least some of the community's habits of life and approaches to Bible reading, and at the same time to hold to a very strong doctrine of *sola scriptura* that is thoroughly faithful to that of Luther and Calvin.

Scripture and preaching

In this description of preaching I intend to bring together a number of topics that have been worked through in earlier sections of this book. Since preaching is one of the most significant moments in the life of the church where Scripture is opened, it is appropriate to think about preaching here at some length, in the light of the doctrine of Scripture.

Two outstanding contemporary factors lead to the significance
of preaching being reduced in the minds of many Christians in the
Western world. First, we have been taught to be suspicious of any
speaker who stands in a position of power. And the sermon, along
with the political campaign speech and the advertising spiel, is one
of the prime examples of a discourse that intends to exercise
power over others. This kind of suspicion of preaching is undeniably well founded. Sincere believers have often been led astray by
persuasive preachers who claimed to be mouthpieces of God and
special channels of the power of the Holy Spirit, but whose teaching came more from their own imaginations than from Scripture.
Even apart from such flagrantly abusive invocations of the Holy
Spirit, the direct identification of the preaching of the Word of
God as *itself* the Word of God, as confessed especially clearly in
the Second Helvetic Confession of 1566, can look too much like a
Protestant forerunner of the excessive Roman claims of papal
infallibility. In some Protestant churches there is what is sometimes called 'the papacy of the pulpit', where preaching tends to
mimic some of the Roman papacy's overwhelming and authoritarian prominence – although of course usually in a more austere
style.

Some preachers, it is true, seeing all these dangers clearly, seek a
mode of preaching that avoids any exercise of power, or any
exalted theological claims for the content of the sermon. In
sermons like these the preacher comes not proclaiming, declaring,
exhorting and rebuking, but sharing, musing, reflecting and imagining. However, this kind of preaching has not generally proved any
more acceptable in the modern world (and in the modern
Christian world) than that which seeks to display power. If the
preacher exercises too much power, he can be fought. If he is too
weak he can be ignored.

The main problem with preaching in this 'weak' style is that it
is not weak for any of the same reasons that the apostle Paul
judged his own preaching to be weak. What Paul called 'weak'
was his decision not to preach in Corinth with rhetorical flourishes or theological speculations, but instead to preach Jesus
Christ and him crucified in simple words, leaving it to the Holy
Spirit to demonstrate to his hearers the truth of his message

(1 Cor. 2:1–5). Preaching that seeks to learn from this exemplary form of 'weakness' should be confident and assertive about what can be known, and what must be proclaimed of God and his ways, because God has revealed it to us. It should also be clear-headed about what cannot be said, because God has not revealed it to us in the same way. Preaching goes as tragically astray when it muses and reflects on those matters it should be proclaiming, as it does when it confidently proclaims what the preacher cannot know, because Scripture is silent.

The second factor that puts preachers on the defensive today is more theological. It is the refusal by some to link God's ongoing dynamic action through the Spirit directly with the speech acts communicated by the words of Scripture (which, I have been arguing throughout, are linked at a fundamental level). In some modern theology the Spirit's contemporary speaking activity is not supremely related to the language and meanings of Scripture. When we want to know what the Spirit says to the church, it is not always supremely to Scripture that we are sent. Instead the 'speech' of the Holy Spirit is transformed into something more metaphorical, and is located in what we think we can identify as the Spirit's wordless guidings and promptings.

A preacher's understanding of the nature of the work of the Holy Spirit in relation to the language and meanings of Scripture profoundly affects his preaching, for better or worse. For example, if as a preacher I am hesitant that the Spirit will come and act supremely through my preaching of the speech acts of Scripture because he once authored them and is alive to speak them again, then my preaching, if it is to be proclamatory, will probably take one of two forms. I might end up recommending my own spiritual experience as normative, perhaps using some biblical texts to illustrate my experience, by way of historical precedent. Or I might focus on rehearsing the beliefs and practices of my Christian sub-culture or denomination, which distinguish us from other groups, with the Bible again reduced to serving as a doctrinal sourcebook, or as a handbook of practical illustrations.

Yet, despite this modern nervousness about identifying the sermon with the word of God, throughout the New Testament it is simply assumed that what the disciples preach really is to be identified with God speaking. As we saw in the biblical outline, Jesus tells the seventy before he sends them out, 'Whoever listens to you listens to me; whoever rejects you rejects me' (Luke 10:16). He tells the Twelve, 'whoever accepts anyone I send accepts me' (John 13:20). Paul claims that God's message of the hope of eternal life is brought to light through his proclamation (Titus 1:3). He commends the Thessalonians for accepting his spoken message not as simply human words, but 'as it actually is, the word of God' (1 Thess. 2:13). He tussles with the Corinthian Christians who were beginning to doubt that his apparently unimpressive style of speech really was to be identified with God's direct speech to them (1 Cor. 1 – 2).[24]

To claim that one's own human speech about Christ crucified really is *God* speaking, and that the Holy Spirit comes in power through one's apparently weak speech, seems to run dangerously close to blasphemy. Yet that is clearly the pattern for the extension of the gospel after Pentecost that Christ and the apostles established. Fraught with dangers and temptations though it is, it is simply given to us as our pattern for ministry. Karl Barth warns preachers that the real question about preaching that they face is not 'How *does* one do it?' but 'How *can* one do it?'[25] The warning he implies in this statement is always apt. The New Testament precedent is simply that the preacher can preach and must preach, fearful and trembling because he is given the privilege of speaking God's words and has no power to determine the result of his preaching, but not so fearful that he loses his resolve to know and proclaim Christ and him crucified.

What guards the preacher from arrogance, and from the blasphemous claim that his own words are the words of God when they are not, is the constant reminder that every aspect of the act of preaching is enabled only by the activity of the Holy Spirit. One of Calvin's regular themes when he discusses preaching and

---

24. See further Donald G. Bloesch, *Essentials of Evangelical Theology*, vol. 2, *Life, Ministry, and Hope* (Peabody: Prince, 1978), pp. 71–103.

25. Karl Barth, *The Word of God and the Word of Man*, tr. Douglas Horton (London: Hodder & Stoughton, n. d.), p. 103.

preachers is that God simultaneously exalts and humbles them. They are set apart by God as ministers of the Spirit, but God claims for himself all the power and efficacy of preaching.[26] I therefore want to explore a little how preachers are surrounded, behind and before, by the activity of the Holy Spirit. It is not just that the Spirit is at work in the actual delivery of a sermon. He has also *gone before* the preacher. At the moment of the delivery of the sermon, the three elements of preaching (the *biblical text* to be preached, the *preacher* himself and the listening *congregation*) all derive their true identity from the work of the Holy Spirit in and on them. They are what they are only by virtue of his work. The sermon is preached in a Spirit-formed and Spirit-infused situation. The powerful activity of the Holy Spirit in the act of preaching itself is therefore not a 'bolt from the blue', where God steps in in power for 10, 20 or 40 minutes. Instead the Spirit's power working through the Word preached is integrally related to and dependent upon the Spirit's preparatory and ongoing work in the biblical text, in the preacher and in the listening people. We need to think a little about the Spirit's preparatory work in each of these three elements.

The Spirit and the Bible

What the Bible says, God says – and God the Holy Spirit has been providentially active in the world to bring this about. It is not that the divine component of Scripture excludes the human, but rather that the divine and human actions function together ('concursively'), as God superintends the production of Scripture. Indeed 'superintends' is one of B. B. Warfield's key terms to describe God's providential action in the authoring and compiling of Scripture.[27] This concept of biblical inspiration is therefore really, as we saw previously, an aspect of the doctrine of providence.

---

26. See esp. John Calvin, Commentary on 1 Cor. 3:7; 2 Cor. 3:6; 1 Pet. 1:25; *Institutes* 4.1.6.

27. See A. N. S. Lane, 'B. B. Warfield on the Humanity of Scripture', *Vox evangelica* 16 (1986), pp. 77–94.

This doctrine of plenary, verbal biblical inspiration provides a great practical benefit for preachers. It gives the preacher an authoritative, meaningful content: a speech act with both propositional content and active purpose. It gives him something to say that is clearly not his own word, and at root not a word of purely human origin, because God has uttered it in advance of him. He can therefore be protected from being a false teacher in the pulpit. The Spirit does not inspire a fresh gospel with every sermon, whose claim to truth could only be related to the person of the preacher. If that were so, we would be lost in the kinds of destructive personality cults that seem to have bedevilled the early Corinthian church, and have affected many other churches since. Instead the Spirit calls both the congregation and the preacher back to the message revealed once for all. The Spirit's activity through the speech acts of the Bible *now* is consistent with his activity in their composition at the level of grammar and meanings *back then*. The Spirit, as the Spirit of Christ, navigates the church into the future by calling it back to the written Word he authored.

Moreover the Spirit has gone before the preacher in the production of Scripture in such a way that the biblical texts give rise to meaning in just the same way as every other human text. Of course much of the content of Scripture is unique to it, and the purpose for which it was written is a purpose only God can bring about, but the way the biblical language functions as language is ordinary and human. The Holy Spirit impresses on the preacher's mind and heart the natural meaning of the Bible's words, in order that he can now preach it, confident that God has given him a message that saves him from blasphemously preaching his own message. This confidence inevitably entails risks, for in sinful people it can easily be transformed into confidence in oneself. But what cannot be avoided is the fact that God chooses that human words should also be the medium of his speech. Calvin notes how often in the Bible there is 'such a connection and bond of union between Christ's grace and man's effort, that in many cases that is ascribed to the minister which belongs exclusively to the Lord'. The preacher can say of his own words 'this is what God says . . .' only because of the Bible's testimony to God's providential action through human action, and because God's action in and through the Bible's speech

acts forms the content of his proclamation. Preaching is an outstanding example of what Calvin calls 'the entire dispensation of
the gospel, which consists, on the one hand, in the secret influence
of Christ, and, on the other, in man's outward efforts'.[28]

In the light of this, what the faithful biblical preacher does, and
what the Holy Spirit does with Scripture through him, is best
described as *a contemporary re-enactment of the speech act that the Spirit
performed in the original authoring of the text*. This notion, that the
sermon is itself a redemptive *act* of God in the present, is
common in literature on preaching. The sermon is an act that continues through time the great redemptive act God performed once
in history in the sending of his Son. P. T. Forsyth, a Scottish theologian of the late nineteenth and early twentieth century, says that
the gospel 'is God's act of redemption before it is man's message
of it . . . And it is this act that is prolonged in the word of the
preacher, and not merely proclaimed.'[29] Calvin's own theory and
practice of preaching have been described in similar terms: 'Calvin
always thinks of preaching as a *traditio*, a handing over of something received; as such, it is a moment in God's reconciliation of
the world unto himself.'[30]

Human and divine activity come together most profoundly in
preaching at this point. A biblical text written, for example, to
instil in its first readers and hearers a confident hope that at the
future coming of Christ their perseverance in the faith will be
vindicated performs that same action again in the lives of con-

28. Calvin, Commentary on 2 Cor. 3:6.

29. P. T. Forsyth, *Positive Preaching and the Modern Mind* (London: Hodder &
    Stoughton, 1907), p. 6. Although in many ways Forsyth was influenced
    by the conclusions of sceptical biblical studies, he makes several
    insightful observations about preaching. On preaching as a redemptive
    act, see also 'Preaching is not merely a word *about* God and his
    redemptive acts but a word *of* God and as such itself a redemptive event'
    (Sidney Greidanus, *The Modern Preacher and the Ancient Text: Interpreting and
    Preaching Biblical Literature* [Grand Rapids: Eerdmans; Leicester: IVP,
    1988], p. 9).

30. T. H. L. Parker, *Calvin's Preaching* (Edinburgh: T. & T. Clark, 1992), p. 36.

temporary believers. It does so in a sermon if the preacher is faithful to the *purpose* of the original text, and fashions his sermon not just as a speech *about* hope, but as *itself* a hope-inspiring action. Some incidental places and practices referred to in Scripture will be modified in the sermon, of course, as the message is applied to contemporary listeners, who live, say, in twenty-first-century Britain and not in ancient Thessalonica. But the text's original Spirit-given *purpose*, and its fundamental meaningful *content* about Christ, his future appearing and the situation of Christian believers in the world will be faithfully re-enacted. The Spirit is again graciously present in the preached message, if what is preached now is faithful in *purpose* and *content* to what he once inspired.

Preaching obviously fails to be faithful to Scripture if it follows Scripture's purpose without being fully shaped by its content. This is typical of preaching in theologically liberal churches, which seeks to give hope and inspire faith, but often proclaims a Christ different from the one found in the New Testament. It can also happen in those more orthodox evangelical circles that place a particularly high value on passion and emotion in their preachers.

Yet preaching also fails to be faithful to Scripture if it follows Scripture's *content* without also seeking to be the vehicle for the re-enactment of the *purpose* for which that content was given. This can happen in some conservative evangelical preaching, especially when the basic model of the preacher is assumed to be that of a 'Bible teacher' (as it often is in the culture in which I have been trained for ministry). Faithful biblical preaching must certainly include exegetical and doctrinal instruction, but it cannot be content with just these things. If it is, it is likely to seem dull and lifeless, lacking the power to move the emotions and the will. Properly faithful biblical preaching involves the preacher deliberately seeking to fashion every verbal (and indeed physical) aspect of his preaching in such a way that the Spirit may *act* through his words in the lives of his hearers, ministering the content of Scripture in accordance with the purpose of Scripture.

The Spirit and the preacher

The Spirit has therefore gone before the preacher and his sermon with regard to the biblical text. He has also gone before the preacher with regard to the preacher himself. First, the faithful biblical preacher should always be someone who has been formed through personal encounter with the Holy Spirit. This is true of both his identity as an individual believer who is in relationship with the risen Christ through the Spirit, as well as his identity as a person gifted by the Holy Spirit as a preacher. The well-known adage that good preaching is 'truth through personality' expresses this point well, as long as it is understood to refer to regenerate personality. The preacher should have grappled with the meaning of the text in his preparation, desiring the Spirit-given purpose of the biblical text to become real in his own life. He should enter the pulpit as someone who has been chastened by the Spirit, or given new hope, or set out on a new course of action, or renounced a kind of behaviour, or had love rekindled in his heart, that is, responding faithfully to the speech act conveyed by the Scripture on which he is preaching. Only if the purpose of the text has been re-enacted by the Spirit in the preacher prior to preaching can he expect to be the means of the same re-enactment by the Spirit in the lives of his hearers. John Goldingay puts it this way: 'In preaching we do not merely report what was once said or relate something we have overheard. Biblical preaching flows from a renewed listening to scripture.'[31] The graciousness of God is evident in the consistency of the Spirit's work through the text. He acts in the preacher's life with the same intention as he did in the original audience, and he acts upon the hearers of the sermon with the same intention as he acted on the preacher.

However, it might be thought that this makes the powerful work of the Holy Spirit through preaching too dependent on the spiritual state of the preacher. Christian experience does suggest that the Holy Spirit sometimes works through the preaching of very ungodly preachers. The Second Helvetic Confession makes this very point in its identification of the sermon with the Word of God: 'the Word itself which is preached is to be regarded, not the minister that preaches; for even if he be evil and a sinner, never-

---

31. John Goldingay, *Models for Interpretation of Scripture* (Grand Rapids: Eerdmans; Carlisle: Paternoster, 1995), p. 278.

theless the Word of God remains still true and good'.[32] Here preaching is regarded in the same way as the sacraments, whose efficacy is independent of the identity or spiritual state of the one who administers them. The apostle Paul's comment in Philippians 1:15–18 comes to mind here. Writing from prison, he says:

> It is true that some preach Christ out of envy and rivalry, but others out of goodwill. The latter do so out of love, knowing that I am put here for the defence of the gospel. The former preach Christ out of selfish ambition, not sincerely, supposing that they can stir up trouble for me while I am in chains. But what does it matter? The important thing is that in every way, whether from false motives or true, Christ is preached. And because of this I rejoice.

In fact, though, Paul says nothing explicit about the efficacy of the preaching of these two different groups of preachers. Moreover, it is very likely that these 'rival' preachers are orthodox Christians, and not heretics or Judaizers, as has sometimes been argued. They are probably part of the group of 'brothers and sisters' to whom Paul refers in verse 14, who have been given, he says, boldness to preach by the news of his imprisonment. In addition, the content of their preaching, despite their opposition to an imprisoned apostle, is still Christ.[33] Despite the strength of Paul's language, what divides the two groups is not that one lives faithfully in obedience to Christ and one does not, but that one sees clearly God's providential hand in Paul's imprisonment and the other is, presumably, embarrassed and ashamed by it, and probably therefore scornful of him. Their failure to see God's hand in Paul's suffering is a serious shortcoming, but it does not seem entirely to invalidate their identity as faithful Christians and preachers.

However, there is other evidence in the New Testament which suggests that the effectiveness of Christian preaching in the power

---

32. Arthur C. Cochrane (ed.), *Reformed Confessions of the 16th Century* (London: SCM, 1966), p. 225.

33. See Peter T. O'Brien, *The Epistle to the Philippians*, New International Greek Testament Commentary (Grand Rapids: Eerdmans, 1991), p. 103.

of the Holy Spirit *is* somewhat dependent on the quality of those who preach. An outstanding example can be found in Paul's testimony to his own preaching ministry in Thessalonica. In 1 Thessalonians 1:4–5 Paul tells the believers, 'we know, brothers and sisters loved by God, that he has chosen you, because our gospel came [*egenēthē*] to you not simply with words but also with power, with the Holy Spirit and deep conviction. You know how we lived [*eegenēthēmen*] among you for your sake.' In Paul's mind the coming of the gospel and his own coming as a faithful Christian believer to Thessalonica are linked. The repetition of *ginomai* as the main verb in verse 5 most likely emphasizes this point.[34] The effect of Paul's preached message was that it transformed the lives of many who heard it into the kind of life lived by the preacher himself. The link between the preacher's life and his preaching as an effective message is all the clearer in these two verses if the 'deep conviction' refers not to the manner of Paul's preaching but to the conviction of the truth of the gospel his preaching brought about in the Thessalonians.[35] This theme is important in 1 Thessalonians: having outlined it in chapter 1, Paul then expands on it in 2:1–12, 17–20. We can therefore say that the Second Helvetic Confession is right, in that the Word preached, if faithful to the Word written, is still the Word of God. However, its effectiveness through the Spirit in people's lives as the Word of God can be hampered if the preacher's life is significantly at odds with the message.

Previously I was critical of the idea that the preacher should present his own spiritual experience as exemplary for the congregation. Yet there *is* something exemplary about the preacher. He

---

34. I owe this observation to my former colleague Andrew Cornes.

35. Commentators disagree on this. F. F. Bruce relates it to the effect
    on the Thessalonians: F. F. Bruce, *1 and 2 Thessalonians*, Word Biblical
    Commentary 45 (Waco: Word, 1982), p. 15. Calvin and Wanamaker
    relate it to Paul's preaching: Charles A. Wanamaker, *The Epistles to the
    Thessalonians*, New International Greek Testament Commentary
    (Grand Rapids: Eerdmans; Carlisle: Paternoster, 1990), pp. 78–79;
    see also Calvin, Commentary on 1 Thess. 1:4–5.

should not proudly witness to his level of attainment in obeying the text. But he may witness to what the Spirit has done in him and to him through the text, and what the Spirit therefore longs to do for others through the text.

The preacher has thus been formed through a personal encounter with the Holy Spirit, acting on and in him through the biblical texts. In addition preachers are formed in Spirit-filled communities. Faithful biblical preachers do not appear out of nowhere, like some modern-day Melchizedek. They are educated, spiritually formed and called as preachers in churches indwelt by the Holy Spirit. When the church calls someone to be a preacher, it acknowledges that it will sit under that person's authority as a preacher. Under the guidance of the Holy Spirit the church has the authority to call the preacher, recognizing that the Spirit will work and speak prophetically through him.

More than that, the preacher should lift people's eyes from the particularities of their own Christian community to the worldwide nature of the gospel they have come to believe. P. T. Forsyth says that 'the preacher's address to the Church is really the Church preaching to the Church. . . . [preaching is] the great, common, universal faith addressing the faith of the local community'.[36] Paul's letters do this on a number of occasions. He reminds small groups of believers that they belong to something bigger than themselves. They did not choose God, but he chose them to be part of the growth of the kingdom of his Son throughout the world. What they believe, hard-pressed though they are, is believed by countless others scattered through the world. Through preaching in this vein, the Spirit reminds the local church that it forms just a part of the great living spiritual house God is building (see 1 Pet. 2:4–5). Through the preacher the Spirit lifts the local church to glimpse the reality of the kingdom he is building in the world, and of which they form a part. Their faith is neither futile nor illusory, because of the reality of the Spirit's universal work.

Preachers, more than all believers, should therefore sit light to denominational distinctives, if the Spirit is to speak fully through

---

36. Forsyth, *Positive Preaching*, pp. 92, 94.

their preaching of his wide-ranging work in the world. This does not mean that they must deny who they and their congregations are. They may need to explain from Scripture (where possible!) the origin of their own denominational distinctives. But preachers should not be defensive about such distinctives, especially when there are other credally orthodox believers who take a different view. (Here we see the significance of the creeds, referred to in the earlier section on *sola scriptura*, to preachers.) The preacher must make clear to the congregation that their allegiance is supremely to every other congregation where the same Spirit of the risen Christ is clearly present and at work.

/0⁻27

The Spirit and the people of God

The Spirit has gone before the preacher in the formation of his preaching text and in his personal formation, both as a Christian believer and as one called to preach the universal gospel to particular congregations. It is also the case that the Spirit has gone before the preacher in the formation of *the people who receive his preaching*. It is the Spirit who has formed this body of people who sit before him. It is only because they walk in step with the Spirit that they will even want to hear what he wants to say. One of the ironies for people who walk in step with the Spirit is that it is only when they are in step with the Spirit that they know they are beginning to slip out of step with him. The best reason for meeting with other Christians is because they want as a body to be called back to faithful, obedient Christian believing and living. In this regard the twentieth-century German writer Dietrich Bonhoeffer once commented on the description in Acts 2:42 that the early believers continued in the apostles' teaching. The essence of teaching, he noted, is usually that it should make itself superfluous, as people learn what is taught. However, with Christian teaching the very thing required is repetition.[37] Until Christ returns, the simultaneously Spirit-filled and sinful church will require such repetition. The church knows its own need of regular preaching only when,

---

37. Dietrich Bonhoeffer, *The Cost of Discipleship* (New York: Touchstone, 1995 [1959]), p. 249.

as the temple of the Holy Spirit, it sees how far short it still falls of the glory of God. The church is already indwelt with the Holy Spirit, but it knows its need to be continually filled with the Spirit, which means to be more aware of and more in line with the reality of the one who really does indwell it.

The preacher with a Christian congregation is therefore not bringing something fundamentally new in his sermon. Of course he should be teaching aspects of the biblical faith they are still unaware of, but he is only bringing to light for them from Scripture what is already true of them, explaining more of the truth that is already theirs. At heart he is reminding them of the one thing that has been undeniably true of them ever since they first devoted themselves to the apostolic gospel: that by the work of the Spirit of God they are not what they once were. The preacher who longs to be a channel of the Spirit's work in people's lives is longing to be such a channel for people in whom the Spirit is already at work, quite apart from his preaching. Thus we can say that in preaching the Spirit speaks through a Spirit-given Word, by means of a Spirit-formed preacher to a Spirit-indwelt people. At every point the preacher is hemmed in by the work and life of the Spirit.

Preaching is the moment of truth in the life of the Christian community. The Spirit who dwells in the people also stands outside them, speaking through the Scriptures he has previously authored, in order to call them to be faithful to the work he has begun in them. The sermon is often the moment in the life of a hard-pressed Christian when she can say, 'Yes, that's what's really true. That's what I really believe.' That happens when the indwelling Spirit opens us up to what the Spirit is saying and doing through the word being preached to us. Preaching is therefore part of the spiritual means by which God sends his Spirit on to and into us, in order to bring us into union with Christ, and to keep us within his covenant people. As the apostle Peter makes clear, God in his glory and goodness has chosen to allow us to participate, as he says, in the divine nature through his 'very great and precious promises' (2 Pet. 1:3–4). As I have said more than once, a promise cannot be conveyed in any other way than by language. It must be spoken, if it is to be an effective promise. We thus come into communion with God through his linguistic communication with us. It is these divine speech acts, given in Scripture, which the preacher is called to proclaim and repeat. In that proclamation and repetition God is present, performing again for the congregation the covenant promise he made in the Scriptures. It is the preacher's privilege that God will choose to use the re-enacting of his divine speech acts in the preacher's sermon as the occasion for bringing people to participate in the divine nature. God certainly acts in that way by the power of his Spirit in the act of preaching itself. He does so only as the climax of a long preparatory action by the Spirit in the formation of Scripture, of the preacher and of the listening congregation.

Scripture and the individual Christian

In a great deal of evangelical culture the reading of Scripture by the individual Christian sits at the heart of the practices that mark out a faithful believer. This has been particularly true of the circles in which I have been educated and formed, and for which I am deeply grateful. It is right for individual Bible reading, as an aspect of Christian discipleship, to be prized, encouraged and taught. Central to the concerns of the Protestant Reformation was the conviction that the Holy Spirit is poured out on *each one* who comes to Christ in faith, and that therefore the Lord establishes a relationship with each one through his Word, in the power of the Spirit. It is of course perfectly possible to overindividualize our understanding of salvation and relationship with Christ, and this has undoubtedly sometimes happened in evangelicalism. However, as earlier sections of this chapter have argued, too strong a stress on individualism is not a necessary feature of Reformation Protestantism. Where it occurs, it is an infiltration of outside cultural influences into the Christian community. Yet it is also possible to overemphasize the corporate aspects of Christian faith, and to make too little of the truth that individuals stand in their own right as responsible to their creator.

Many Christians in poorer parts of the world rightly yearn to have what Western Christians have long since taken for granted: ready access to Scripture for themselves in their own home, in a reliable translation in their own language. Western Christians should count their possession of these riches as a particular blessing. (I would not be the first to point out that it might be better if money invested in fine-tuning yet more niche-market Bible translations in English were spent instead on getting good translations into the hands of our brothers and sisters throughout the world who as yet have no serviceable Bible to hand.) As Article 24 of the Anglican Thirty-Nine Articles asserts, public prayer and liturgy, alongside Scripture, should never be 'in a tongue not understood of the people', for such a thing would be 'plainly repugnant to the Word of God'.

There are two issues for us to think through about the relationship of the individual Christian to Scripture, in the light of the kind of doctrine of Scripture I have been outlining. The first is the relationship between the private reading of Scripture, on the one hand, and its corporate reading and preaching, on the other. The second asks what the believer's aim and goal should be in the reading of Scripture.

D-29

Private Bible reading in relation to corporate Bible reading and preaching

There are many contemporary Christians who prize one of these over the other. Some are happy to lap up teaching and preaching in meetings and conferences, seeing little need also to open up Scripture privately for themselves. Others regard the preaching of Scripture in the church as essentially something over which they sit in judgment, discerning whether or not it accords with what they confidently feel the Lord has said to them in their personal reading of Scripture. I would suggest that the healthiest way to relate the two is to think of the individual reading of Scripture as derivative of, and dependent on, the corporate reading and proclamation of Scripture in the Christian assembly.[38]

There are two key reasons for relating the individual to the corporate in this way. First, we cannot ignore the fact that the church

---

38. Mark Thompson makes the same point: Mark D. Thompson, *A Clear and Present Word: The Clarity of Scripture* (Leicester: Apollos, 2006), p. 120.

is the primary means God has given us for coming to encounter him in his Word in a way that enables us to hear his voice and respond to him. As we have seen above, this observation is not commonly made in modern popular evangelicalism, perhaps because it can begin to sound 'too Catholic' to some, and a betrayal of the Protestant heritage. However, as we also saw, if we do grant this significant role to the church, we are rather more in line with the consistent views of the church fathers and the Protestant Reformers than modern evangelicalism often is.

The public reading and preaching of Scripture should give those who hear it both a structure and some tools that will enable their private reading of Scripture to be faithful to Scripture, without distorting it. For good preaching will constantly focus on the primary truths God teaches in Scripture. In that way it gives hearers a regular indication of the main teachings they should expect to encounter in their own Bible reading. I remember noticing, as a new convert and a young man, that the same teachings emerged again and again in the preaching from Scripture I was hearing. These were the Bible's fundamental teachings, as expressed in the historic creeds. Over the course of a year it dawned on me that those truths must be fundamental to Scripture, and must govern my personal interpretation of it. In this sense, good preaching exercises something of a 'credal' function in the local church, giving people an interpretative structure in which to make sense of individual parts of Scripture when they encounter them for themselves.

As well as a structure for understanding Scripture, a good preacher will also give his hearers tools by which they can learn to interpret Scripture faithfully for themselves. How do we interpret apocalyptic literature? How do we understand Old Testament prophecies and Old Testament laws in the light of Christ? What do we do when it seems to us that one part of Scripture contradicts another? How do people grow in knowledge and understanding of Scripture when there is so much of it that as yet they cannot make sense of for themselves? (And so on.) Of course Christians can learn these things through reading books for themselves, but they are best taught by their own pastor-teachers in the local congregation.

Giving priority to the corporate use of Scripture over the individual, in this way, recognizes that the Lord continues to give his church pastor-teachers who will expound the biblical writings of the prophets and apostles, in order to equip his people for works of service, and to build up the body of Christ (as Paul puts it in Eph. 4:11–13). This perhaps ought to give Christians a reason for aligning at least some of their personal reading of Scripture more closely with the texts they hear preached than they are accustomed to doing.

A second reason for making the individual reading of the Bible dependent on its corporate reading and exposition is the fact that Scripture has been read, prayed over, wrestled with, talked about and taught for two millennia before any of us were born. Those millennia have produced settled convictions about the Bible's most significant teachings, as well as reliable practices of interpretation. Our primary attitude towards these things ought humbly to be that of a learner, not a critic.

One small illustration of this point might help. I have sometimes been encouraged by others, both as a preacher and as a Christian who reads Scripture for myself, only to turn to Bible commentaries as a very last resort, when, after much wrestling and searching for myself, I still could not make out the sense of a passage – or perhaps just to check that what I thought was its meaning was not entirely off-beam. There is certainly merit in not simply turning to learned books to find 'the answers', as a lazy short-cut to avoid wrestling with Scripture for myself. Yet increasingly, when reading Scripture, I find myself wanting to turn to a good Bible commentary sooner rather than later. My reason is this: a good commentary will give me an insight into the consensus view on the meaning of each passage held by the generations of believers who have come before me. Working within that framework seems to be a sensible, humble and faithful place to start. For most Christians, who lack the time, resources and perhaps also the inclination to do the research themselves, good preaching will be a crucial means by which that historic consensus on Scripture's meaning is conveyed to individual believers. For that, of course, the preacher needs to be, as he should be, well educated in biblical, historical and systematic theology.

Nothing that I have just said denies outright that God can cause new light to break out from Scripture, enabling us to see truths in it that our forebears did not. Nor am I denying that the Lord can speak through Scripture to individuals privately, teaching them and acting on them in such a way that they become the tools in his hand for the reformation of existing practices and beliefs in the wider church. Part of the truth of the sixteenth-century Reformation is precisely that God did this, and it is certainly not the only time he has done it. Yet it is only part of the truth. It is equally true (probably more so) that the Lord enabled the Reformers to put into practice both traditional beliefs about Scripture stretching back right to the early days of the church, and also inherited ways of interpreting and applying Scripture, all of which had been obscured but never lost. That is certainly how Luther and Calvin themselves understood what they were doing.

The aim of Bible reading

The second issue that must concern us here is this: What should Christians' aims be when they open the Bible to read it for themselves? The answer to this question is of course no different from what Christians' aims should be when they hear the Bible preached. What we expect from Scripture must be determined entirely by what Scripture is, and the purpose for which God has caused it to be written. As I have been saying throughout this book, the words of Scripture are the vehicle for God's speech, and consequently the speech acts of Scripture are God in communicative action. In Scripture, God presents himself to us, making his covenant promise to us. As part of that overall action, he performs many subsidiary actions through Scripture: eliciting faith, warning, rebuking, encouraging, provoking hope, motivating to repentance and holiness and so on. And, as a necessary feature of all these actions, God teaches us truths about himself, ourselves, the past and the future. Thus Scripture, like all spoken or written language, is made up of propositional content and authorial purpose, and the two ought never to be separated if we wish to hear what God is saying in Scripture.

Therefore the most appropriate question to ask ourselves when we open Scripture to read it is: *What is God wanting to do* to *me, and* in *me, through the words I am reading?* When we read the Bible we must be ready, in the first instance, for God to *act* on us and in us. For, as we encounter his words, and as we encounter the actions he performs by means of them, we are encountering God himself.

It is important to be clear that this is not opening up the possibility for someone to read a portion of Scripture, and merely declare that they find God doing such and such to them through it. God's acts through Scripture are his *speech* acts. What that act will be is determined entirely by the words themselves, and their semantic content. The norms of grammatical and historical interpretation are not avoided. But interpretation is not an end in itself; reading the Bible is not fundamentally a comprehension exercise. Interpretation should serve only to lead us to an encounter with God as he actually presents himself to us in Scripture.

Thus an individual reading of Scripture must also ask: What is the Lord teaching me here? If we do not ask that question, we shall very likely make individual phrases in Scripture mean what we would like them to mean, regardless of what God has made them mean in the Scriptures he authored. In so doing we shall turn Scripture into an idol that simply reflects our own desires and prejudices. But if our reading of Scripture stops there, asking only about what Scripture 'teaches', our reading has made the mistake of exalting Scripture's content over its purpose. It has ripped apart in Scripture two things that ought not to be ripped apart. Therefore we must also ask: And what, in this part of Scripture, is the Lord wanting to *do* with that teaching, to me and in me?

Many evangelicals worry about 'getting Scripture wrong'. Of course we should be concerned to interpret the meaning of Scripture well, for every believer should be growing in knowledge and understanding of Scripture. However, our greater concern should be the ease with which we can content ourselves with *learning* the truth, while refusing to let God act in us with that truth as the sharp sword he intended it to be. If we want to know what we should do when we read the Bible, our answer is found in asking: What should I do when I encounter words spoken by God – words by which he presents himself to me as a Lord to be known and trusted?

The doctrine of Scripture I have been outlining in this book therefore teaches us that our basic attitude to Scripture should be humility. We should submit our thoughts, hopes and desires to God's thoughts and his will, which he communicates to us in Scripture. We should set aside what seems to us to be true, in order to listen to the truthful and life-giving word of God. This, said Herman Bavinck, 'has been the attitude of the church toward Scripture down the centuries'.[39]

One final comment is in order here. In saying these things about the Bible I do not want to be misunderstood. I am not saying that a believer's relationship with the Lord is only properly 'alive' when he or she reads the Bible or listens to a sermon. There are many occasions when the Lord graciously reminds believers of aspects of his character through events he causes to come into their lives. There are many ways in which he works in people's lives through words someone else says to them, that strike them as particularly pertinent or prophetic, or through strong feelings, impressions and urgings he gives them. In not mentioning these things in this book I have not been denying them or pouring cold water on them. They have simply not been the concern of a relatively short book on Scripture.

What is my concern, though, is that none of these things, valu-able though they are in their own right, should come to be the place where Christians finally rest their assurance of their know-ledge of God, or the place they go first when they are eager to hear the voice of God. For the one place where the voice of God, and therefore what I have called 'the semantic presence of God', may always reliably be found, is in his speaking and acting in the words of Scripture.

---

39. Bavinck, *Reformed Dogmatics*, vol. 1, p. 441.

6. SUMMARY

The central biblical, theological and doctrinal arguments of this book can be summarized briefly.

Scripture, by which we mean the speech acts performed by means of the words of Scripture, is the primary means by which God presents himself to us, in such a way that we can know him and remain in a faithful relationship with him. Once we are clear on this definition of the nature of Scripture, we can say something important and true, even though at first sight it seems perhaps dangerously close to making an idol of the Bible: Scripture is God in communicative action. Therefore to encounter the words of Scripture is to encounter God in action.

Theologically Scripture is the means by which the Father presents his covenant to us, and therefore the means by which he presents himself to us as the faithful God of the covenant. It is also in the words of Scripture that the Word of God, Jesus Christ, comes to us so that we may know him and remain in him. And it is through the Scripture, which he authored, preserved and now illumines, that the Holy Spirit speaks to us most reliably. All this is what we are saying when we confess, simply, that 'The Bible is the Word of God.'

Doctrinally Scripture is necessary, because of the character of God, and because of the covenantal form in which he chooses to relate to us. It is sufficient as the form in which God's covenant promise is made to us. It is clear, in that God's voice speaking through Scripture gives us sufficiently solid grounds to base on Scripture alone our knowledge of God, our trust in him, our hope and our actions. All of this amounts to an exposition of what it means to say that Scripture is authoritative, since to speak of Scripture's authority is really shorthand for speaking of the way in which the sovereign God chooses to speak authoritatively to us in and through Scripture.

Three closing comments seem appropriate. First, all of this is only an outline, recommending the foundational shape the doctrine of Scripture ought to take. Someone may take issue with the foundations for the doctrine I am recommending; if they do, they have at least understood what I am attempting. However, to judge that I have dealt too sketchily with one issue or another is probably to look for more than I have intended to offer.

Secondly, every student of the doctrine of Scripture would do well to read the primary work on Scripture of each of the four writers to whom I referred in the introduction, and to whose work I have regularly appealed. Their writings represent some of the best historic expositions of the evangelical doctrine of Scripture:

1. John Calvin, *Institutes of the Christian Religion*, Book 1.
2. Francis Turretin, *Institutes of Elenctic Theology*, Second Topic: The Holy Scriptures.
3. B. B. Warfield, *The Inspiration and Authority of the Bible*.
4. Herman Bavinck, *Reformed Dogmatics*, vol. 1, *Prolegomena* – Part IV: Revelation.

Greater first-hand knowledge of works such as these among evangelicals would save many from expounding and defending the orthodox doctrine of Scripture in a superficial or unattractive way. It might also prevent some from departing from orthodoxy without ever having encountered the richness and vitality of the evangelical doctrine of Scripture.

Finally, the question remains of how the kind of doctrine of Scripture I am proposing relates to these inherited traditions of evangelical and Reformed teaching about the Bible. Some may suspect that it is simply an old doctrine, say that of Warfield or Turretin, smartened up with a little superficial contemporary theological and philosophical adornment, to face the twenty-first century. Others may feel that this kind of doctrine represents a substantive theological move away, in one way or another, from earlier writing on Scripture, and thereby loses things of real value. My intention, at least, is to offer a faithful reworking, in the light of Scripture, of the orthodox doctrine of Scripture which the majority of believers have held dear through most of the church's history, while casting it in terms that may help to make that doctrine more obviously essential to healthy Christian thought and life in the present.

For the great revealed truth we must trust, explain and defend is that the one who is the Word of life (1 John 1:1) speaks to us words of life (John 6:68). He gives us Scripture as our word of life: the trustworthy, clear and sufficient means of knowing him and remaining in covenant relationship with him, in the power of the Holy Spirit, right up until the day we shall no longer need it, because then we shall see face to face.

INDEX OF ANCIENT AND MODERN
AUTHORS

Abraham, W., 13, 84
Achtemeier, P., 84
Aquinas, 109
Athanasius, 107
Augustine, 107–108, 118,
    144–145, 146
Austin, J., 57

Barr, J., 84
Barth, K., 61–63, 64, 65, 159
Barton, J., 10–11
Basil of Caesarea, 108, 144–145
Bavinck, H., 18, 36, 51, 52,
    71, 72, 73–74, 83, 85, 102,
    105, 128, 138, 144, 150, 176,
    178
Berkouwer, G., 107, 119
Bonhoeffer, D., 168

Calvin, J., 14, 18, 67, 80, 82, 86,
    93, 94, 98–101, 110–111, 142,
    146, 159–160, 161–162, 174,
    178

Derrida, J., 63
Dever, M., 154

Erasmus, 115–118, 122

Forsyth, P., 162, 167

Gadamer, H.-G., 105
Geiselmann, J., 147
Goldingay, J., 44, 164
Greidanus, S., 162
Grudem, W., 124–126

Hagner, D., 43
Hanson, R., 144
Hauerwas, S., 155
Heppe, H., 82
Horton, M., 33

Irenaeus, 118

Jensen, P., 54

Kelly, J., 143
Klauber, M., 120–121
Kline, M., 53

Lane, A., 88, 160
Lessing, G., 40

Luther, M., 115–118, 122, 127,
    142, 174

Macleod, D., 70, 135
McConville, G., 35–36
McGowan, A., 135, 137
McKim, D., 81
Mathison, K., 146–147, 148–149
Metzger, B., 46
Muller, R., 15, 102, 113, 119, 120

Nelson, R., 23
Noll, M., 132

Oberman, H., 144, 145, 147

Packer, J., 18, 70, 75, 136–137
Pannenberg, W., 45
Parker, T., 162
Preus, R., 15

Ricoeur, P., 63, 105
Rogers, J., 81

Schleiermacher, F., 111
Searle, J., 57
Spinoza, B., 40, 111

Tavard, G., 147
Tertullian, 142–143
Thiselton, A., 57, 127
Thompson, M., 115, 124–126,
    171
Trembath, K., 43
Trueman, C., 15, 67
Turretin, F., 18, 71, 92–93,
    101–104, 106, 119,
    125–127, 152–153,
    178

Vanhoozer, K., 57, 63, 64,
    65, 105–106
Vawter, B., 88
Vincent of Lérins, 108,
    118

Ward, T., 13, 57, 63, 64
Warfield, B., 18, 69, 81–83,
    88, 134, 160, 178
Watson, F., 57
Webster, J., 13, 50, 76–77
Wenham, J., 11
Wolterstorff, N., 33, 57–58
Woodbridge, J., 81, 132
Work, T., 22, 30

INDEX OF BIBLICAL REFERENCES

OLD TESTAMENT

Genesis
1 *21, 38*
1:26 *34*
2:17 *21, 26*
2:24 *25–26*
3 *21–22*
3:15 *22*
5:5 *27*
9:8–17 *22*
12:1–3 *23, 27–28*
45:8 *88*

Exodus
6:8 *28*
12:24–28 *30*
17:14 *100*
19:3–6 *28–29*
24:7 *54*
25:10–22 *29*

Numbers
22 *35*

Deuteronomy
18:15–20 *35*
29:29 *117*

2 Samuel
6 *29*
24:1 *139*

1 Kings
13 *23–24*

1 Chronicles
21:1 *139*

2 Chronicles
34:30 *54*

Job
1 – 2 *139*
38 – 41 *32*

Psalms
29 *24*
119:1 *107*
119:105 *101*
119:130 *117*

Isaiah
55:10–11 *24–25*

Jeremiah
1:9–10 *35*
31:31–34 *53*
31:34 *103*
36 *35–36*

Ezekiel
43:11 *100–101*

NEW TESTAMENT

Matthew
5:17 *54*
5:17–18 *86*
10:14–15 *42*
10:40 *42*
12:3–5 *74*
19:4–5 *69, 74*
21:16 *74*
21:42 *74*

22:31 *74*
23 *73*
23:8 *71, 103*
25:31–46
    42–43

Mark
5:41 *90*
7:18–19 *44*
10:46 *139*

Luke
1:1–4 *75*
1:4 *100*
10:16 *159*
18:31 *54*
18:35 *139*
23:43 *53*

John
1:1 *67*
5:19 *37*
6:63 *39*
6:67–69 *39*
6:68 *179*
8:28 *38*
10:34–35 *70*
12:49–50 *38*
13:20 *159*
14:9–11 *37*
15:4–8 *69–70*
16:12–15 *46–48, 70,*
    80
17:8 *38, 42*
17:20 *42*

Acts
1:1 *70*

2:23 *88*
2:42 *168*
4:31 *68*
6:2 *68*
8:4 *68*
8:14 *68*
8:30–35 *126*

Romans
1:18–20 *98*
5–6 *41*
5:8 *25*
8:30 *26*
9:17 *69*

1 Corinthians
1–2 *159*
1:24 *37*
2:1–5 *157–158*
2:6–16 *92*
2:14 *116*
2:20–25 *40*
7:14 *123*
10:1–13 *55*

2 Corinthians
3:12–4:6 *92*

Ephesians
2:20 *43, 101,*
    151
4:11–13 *173*

Philippians
1:15–18 *165*

Colossians
1:19 *37*

2:12 *123*
3:3 *72*

1 Thessalonians
1:4–5 *166*
2:13 *68, 159*

1 Timothy
3:15 *151, 152*

2 Timothy
2:2 *48*
3:14 *48*
3:15 *107*
3:16 *79, 80–84,*
    113

Titus
1:1 *131*
1:2 *133*
1:3 *159*

Hebrews
4:1–13 *55*
4:12 *12*
5:13–14 *101*
6:18 *133*
7:23–8:13
    53

1 Peter
1:23 *101*
2:4–5 *167*

2 Peter
1:3–4 *169*
1:20–21 *79*
3:15–16 *91*

1 John
1:1–2 *39, 72,*
    179
2:27 *103*
5:13 *100*

Jude
3 *102*

Revelation
22:3–5 *72*

22:18 *48*
22:18–20 *107*